Shak

The Golfer's Companion

)

Shakespeare

The Golfer's Companion

A poor player, that struts and frets his hour upon the stage

Shakespeare

The Golfer's Companion

By Syd Pritchard

© Copyright 2005 Syd Pritchard.
All rights reserved. No part of this publication may be reproduced, stored in a retrieval system, or transmitted, in any form or by any means, electronic, mechanical, photocopying, recording, or otherwise, without the written prior permission of the author.

Note for Librarians: A cataloguing record for this book is available from Library and Archives Canada at www.collectionscanada.ca/amicus/index-e.html
ISBN 1-4120-5476-1

Printed in Victoria, BC, Canada. Printed on paper with minimum 30% recycled fibre. Trafford's print shop runs on "green energy" from solar, wind and other environmentally-friendly power sources.

TRAFFORD
PUBLISHING™
Offices in Canada, USA, Ireland and UK
This book was published *on-demand* in cooperation with Trafford Publishing. On-demand publishing is a unique process and service of making a book available for retail sale to the public taking advantage of on-demand manufacturing and Internet marketing. On-demand publishing includes promotions, retail sales, manufacturing, order fulfilment, accounting and collecting royalties on behalf of the author.

Book sales for North America and international:
Trafford Publishing, 6E–2333 Government St.,
Victoria, BC v8t 4p4 CANADA
phone 250 383 6864 (toll-free 1 888 232 4444)
fax 250 383 6804; email to orders@trafford.com
Book sales in Europe:
Trafford Publishing (uk) Limited, 9 Park End Street, 2nd Floor
Oxford, UK oxi 1hh UNITED KINGDOM
phone 44 (0)1865 722 113 (local rate 0845 230 9601)
facsimile 44 (0)1865 722 868; info.uk@trafford.com
Order online at:
trafford.com/05-0374

10 9 8 7 6 5 4

CONTENTS

Chapter

The Golfer's Companion

Preface

In 1985 the author wrote a satirical book, which he called 'A Golfer's Guide To Shakespeare'. At the time he was under the impression that the notion of Shakespeare having been a golfer was a revolutionary one. Subsequently, and largely through its publication he learned of a tract written a century earlier advancing a similar claim. It is understood that this book was either written or published, or both, by David Douglas and entitled 'Shakespeare On Golf' It has an introduction which begins, 'All the world knows that Shakespeare was its one universal genius but probably few have as yet realised his extraordinary knowledge of sport or the extent of his acquaintance with games'.

(The full text of this introduction is included in 'The Companion' as an appendix) Some of the quotations used in the Douglas book have inevitably filtered through to The Golfer's Companion, as have others from various sources, together with a liberal sprinkling from 'A Golfer's Guide'.

In recognising these sources the author is also well aware that 'The Companion' has far from exhausted the golfing references, however tenuous within the pages of the Complete Works of the Bard, the source and inspiration for us all.

A Foreword

The Companion features forty-two broad aspects of golf, each with its own chapter. Each aspect has an introduction preparing the reader for a varying number of quotations which are serious, flippant, or have double meanings. Where it is felt to be helpful the quotation has a lead-in; otherwise the reader is left to interpret as he will.

A book to be dipped into for fun or to provide a ready reference source for the apt witticism, pertinent quip, or serious comment.

A key word index is appended for rapid reference.

*As to text references the precise line number will vary slightly depending on which publication of the play is used.

Chapter 1: The Golf Lesson

There is an obvious and compelling need in golf for the teaching professional. From the numerous references in the plays of W S it is clear that he recognised the value of these highly respected functionaries on the golf scene. Only one dissenting voice is to be found "Throw physic to the dogs, I'll none of it" (Macbeth)

The demand is urgent
> *The need we have to use you did provoke*
> *Our hasty sending.*

[Hamlet II ii 3]

Plenty of customers?
> *Ay, sir, there are a crew of wretched souls*
> *That stay his cure.*

[Macbeth IV iii 141]

Feverish pleas for help
> *Canst thou not,*
> *Pluck from the memory a rooted sorrow.*
> *Raze out the written troubles of the brain,*
> *And with some sweet oblivious antidote*
> *Cleanse the stuff'd bosom of that perilous stuff*
> *Which weighs upon the heart ?*

[Macbeth V iii 42]

The pro's initial reactions
> *This is a sorry sight.*

[Macbeth II ii 21]

Hopeless cases
> *More needs she the divine*
> *Than the physician.*

[Macbeth V i 72]

She's desperate to do well
> *O step between her and her fighting soul.*

[Hamlet III iv 112]

Be gentle
> *Tenderly apply to her some remedies.*

[The Winter's Tale III ii 148]

There are limits to what a man can do
> *This disease is beyond my practice.*

[Macbeth V i 57]

11

Timing's gone to pot
> *Like sweet bells jangled, out of tune and harsh.*

> [Hamlet III i 158]

The Pro's laments
> *The time is out of joint. O cursed spite*
> *That ever I was born to set it right!*

> [Hamlet I v 188]

> *Great griefs, I see, med'cine the less.*

> [Cymbeline IV ii 243]

Buying time
> *At our more considered time we'll read,*
> *Answer, and think upon this business.*

> [Hamlet II ii 82]

The delay could be fatal
> *The patient dies while the physician sleeps.*

> [Rape of Lucrece]

Towards a Diagnosis
> *These profound heaves you must translate;*
> *'Tis fit we understand them.*

> [Hamlet IV v 2]

> *Th'attempt, and not the deed, confounds us.*

> [Macbeth II ii 10]

> *Why I do trifle thus with his despair*
> *Is done to cure it.*

> [King Lear IV vi 32]

About to throw in the towel
> *This visitation*
> *Is but to whet thy almost blunted purpose.*

> [Hamlet III iv 109]

Fundamental remodeling of swing needed
> *Diseases desperate grown*
> *By desperate appliance are reliev'd,*
> *Or not at all.*

> [Hamlet IV iii 9]

We might just cure it in time
> *A little fire is quickly trodden out,*
> *Which, being suffered, rivers cannot quench.*

> [Henry VI Pt.III IV viii 7]

Swinging imagery

> Let's carve him as a dish fit for the gods,
> Not hew him as a carcase fit for hounds.

[Julius Caesar II i 173]

We 're half way there

> The nature of the sicknesss found
> What is the remedy?

[Troilus and Cressida I iii 14]

Let me show you

> He took me by the wrist, and held me hard;
> Then goes he to the length of all his arm,
> And with his other hand thus o'er his brow,
> He falls to such perusal of my face
> As 'a would draw it.

[Hamlet II i 87]

Pro's patience finally snaps

> Turn, hell-hound, turn!.

[Macbeth V viii 4]

One last desperate attempt

> At last, a little shaking of mine arm,
> And thrice his head waving up and down,
> He raised a sigh so piteous and profound
> As it did seem to shatter all his bulk
> And end his being. That done, he lets me go,
> And with his head over his shoulder turn'd,
> He seemed to find his way without his eyes.

[Hamlet II i 93]

Teacher unhinged by failure

> Th'observ'd of all observers- quite, quite down!

[Hamlet III i 154]

> O, woe is me. T'have seen what I have seen,
> See what I see!

[Hamlet III i 160]

Pupil shares teacher's frustration

> If to do were as easy as to know what were good to do,
> Chapels had been churches,
> And poor men's cottages princes' palaces.

[Merchant Of Venice I ii 11]

But expresses appreciation

I shall th'effect of this good lesson keep
As watchman to my heart.

[Hamlet I iii 45]

Should have sought help earlier

That gentle physic given in time had cur'd me;
But now I am past all comforts here, but prayers.

[Henry VIII IV ii 122]

Testimonials

He tells me he hath found
The head and source of your distemper.

[Hamlet II ii 54]

A gifted teacher

At his touch ,
Such sanctity hath heaven given his hand,
They presently amend.

[Macbeth IV iii 143]

The Pro's private thoughts

I can easier teach twenty what were good to be done
Than to be one of the twenty to follow my own teaching.

[The Merchant of Venice I ii 14]

Too self- critical?

We but teach bloody instructions, which badly taught return
To plague the inventor.

[Macbeth I vii 8]

The Pro on trial

Say from whence you owe this strange intelligence.
Speak, I charge you.

[Macbeth I iii 76]

Come, give us a taste of your quality.

[Hamlet II ii 424]

Come clean

It is a good divine that follows his own instructions.

[Merchant Of Venice I ii 13]

And practise what you preach

Do not as some ungracious pastors do,
Show me the steep and thorny way to heaven,
Whiles, like a puff'd and reckless libertine,
Himself the primrose path of dalliance treads,
And recks not his own rede.

[Hamlet I iii 47]

Chapter 2: Hazards

As defined in the Rules of Golf, "A hazard is any bunker or water hazard". To the average golfer, including W.S., this is a woefully inadequate representation of the whole minefield of booby-traps awaiting the unwary golfer of whatever persuasion. Should he be bold, cautious, or of a careless disposition is of little matter. The elements too are bound to put in their own three penn'orth of woe. So, if you can stand it, 'burn' your way through this litany, along with Lear, Hamlet and the rest.

Lamentations

> *Had I but died an hour before this chance,*
> *I had lived a blessed time.*
>
> [Macbeth II iii 91]
>
> *Come weep with me- past hope, past cure, past help.*
>
> [Romeo and Juliet IV i 45]

And more!

> *Lamentings heard i'th'air, strange screams of death,*
> *And prophesying with accents terrible.*
>
> [Macbeth II iii 54]

Pleas for help

> *Is there no pity sitting in the clouds*
> *That sees into the bottom of my grief?*
>
> [Romeo and Juliet III v 198]

A tearful approach

> *Lend me ten thousand eyes,*
> *And I will fill them with prophetic tears.*
>
> [Troilus and Cressida II ii 101]

Bunkered

> *What is this quintessence of dust?*
>
> [Hamlet II ii 316]

You've guessed it

> *Where sighs and groans*
> *And shrieks that rend the air are made.*
> *Where violent sorrow seems a modern ecstasy.*
>
> [Macbeth IV iii 167]

I'll never get out of here

> Here, here will I remain,
> O here will I set up my everlasting rest
> And shake the yoke of inauspicious stars
> From this world-wearied flesh.

[Romeo and Juliet V iii 109]

Help from friends

> Here in the sands, thee I'll rake up.

[King Lear IV vi 270]

A tinge of regret

> And we have done but greenly
> In hugger-mugger to inter him.

[Hamlet IV v 80]

Watery graves

> I'll cross it though it blast me.

[Hamlet I i 127]

> Sweets to the sweet, Farewell.

[Hamlet V i 265]

> Too much water hast thou
> Therefore I forbid my tears.

[Hamlet IV vii 186]

One damned thing after another

> One woe doth tread upon another's heel
> So fast they follow.

[Hamlet IV vii 163]

> Out of the smoke into the smother.

[As You Like It I ii 266]

> When sorrows come,
> They come not single spies
> But in battalions!

[Hamlet IV v 75]

> I have supped full with horrors.

[Macbeth V v 12]

The thicket dilemma

> Lost in a thorny wood
> Seeking a way out, and straying from the way,
> Not knowing how to find the open air.

[Henry IV. Pt III III ii 174]

Tut tut!

> *I'll free myself*
> *Or hew my way out with a bloody axe.*

[Henry VI Pt.III. III ii 179]

Philosophical resignation

> *When remedies are past the griefs are ended.*

[Othello I iii 202]

Are you sure?

> *Treason has done his worst*
> *Nothing can touch him further.*

[Macbeth III ii 2]

Inflationary consequencies

> *A plague of sighings and grief*
> *It blows a man up like a bladder.*

[Henry IV Pt.I II iv 36]

Tactical surrender

> *Our enemies have beat us to the pit:*
> *It is more worthy to leap in ourselves*
> *Than tarry till they push us.*

[Julius Caesar V v 22]

The dying embers of defiance

> *You think I'll weep. No I'll not weep.*
> *I have full cause for weeping,*
> *But this heart shall break*
> *Into a thousand flaws or ere I'll weep.*

[King Lear I iv 280]

Signs of weakening

> *My particular grief is of so flood-gate*
> *And o'er bearing a nature that it engluts*
> *And swallows other sorrows.*

[Othello I iii 55]

> *So weary with disasters*
> *That I would set my life on any chance*
> *To mend it or be rid on't.*

[Macbeth III i 108]

That's for sure!

> *The worst is death*
> *And death will have his day.*

[Richard III. III ii 103]

But time's a great healer

> *And all these present woes shall serve*
> *For sweet discourses in our time to come.*

[Romeo and Juliet II v 52]

Chapter 3: Gamesmanship

Call it golf psychology if you like; one-upmanship, part of the sub-culture of lifemanship and the brainchild of Stephen Potter pervades all aspects of the golf game. It ranges from the scrupulous application of the rules (in your own interests, of course) to coming within a hair's breadth of downright cheating.

The wily W.S. as you might suspect was well aware of the full gamut. He even invented some of the more subtle stratagems. But whether he used them to win matches is a matter of scurrilous speculation.

Simulated grief at opponent's misfortune

> *With devotion's visage and pious action*
> *We do sugar o'er the devil himself.*
>
> > [Hamlet III i 47]
>
> *To show an unfelt sorrow is an office*
> *Which the false man does easy.*
>
> > [Macbeth II iii 125]
>
> *My tears begin to take his part so much*
> *They mar my counterfeiting.*
>
> > [King Lear III vi 60]
>
> *False face must hide what the false heart doth know.*
>
> > [Macbeth I vii 82]
>
> *0 what a goodly outside falsehood hath.*
>
> > [Merchant of Venice I iii 99]

More dissembling

> *Bear welcome in your eye, your hand, your tongue;*
> *Look like the innocent flower,*
> *But be the serpent under't.*
>
> > [Macbeth I v 63]
>
> *Let not our looks put on our purpose.*
>
> > [Julius Caesar II i 225]
>
> *Look how we can or sad or merrily*
> *Interpretation will misquote our looks.*
>
> > [Henry 1V Pt.I V ii 8]
>
> *The seeming truth which cunning times put on*
> *To entrap the wisest.*
>
> > [The Merchant of Venice III ii 97]

Disguised talent

> *Have more than thou showest*
> *Speak less than thou knowest*
> *And thou shalt have more*
> *Than two tens to a score.*

[King Lear I iv 117]

Honeyed words

> *In law what plea so tainted and corrupt*
> *But being season'd with a gracious voice*
> *Obscures the show of evil.*

[The Merchant of Venice III ii 73]

> *Give thy thoughts no tongue,*
> *Nor any unproportioned thought his act.*
> *Give every man thine ear but few thy voice .*
> *Take every man's censure but reserve thy judgement.*

[Hamlet I iii 59]

Coded language

> *By the pricking of my thumbs*
> *Something wicked this way comes.*

[Macbeth I i 44]

Keeping one step ahead

> *Who is so gross that cannot see this palpable device,*
> *But who so bold that says he sees it not.*

[Richard III III vi 9]

Striking when the moment is right

> *Thoughts black, hands apt, drugs fit and time agreeing.*

[Hamlet III ii 248]

> *I'll observe his looks,*
> *I'll tent him to the quick,*
> *If he but blench I know my course.*

[Hamlet II ii 592]

> *There is a tide in the affairs of men,*
> *Which taken at the flood,*
> *Leads on to fortune.*

[Julius Caesar IV iii 217]

> *Now might I do it pat, now he is praying.*

[Hamlet III iii 73]

> *And what needful else we will perform*
> *In measure time and place.*

[Macbeth V viii 71]

Flatter to deceive
> *The less they deserve,*
> *The more merit is in thy bounty.*

[Hamlet II ii 526]

Pile on the compliments
> *Worse than the sun in March*
> *This praise doth nourish agues.*

[Henry IV Pt.1 V i 11]

Spare me your talk of morality
> *Conscience is a word that cowards use.*

[Richard III V iii 309]

Convince opponent you're on his side really
> *Assume a virtue if you have it not.*

[Hamlet III iv 188]

Respond with feeling to his misfortune
> *Praising what is lost*
> *Makes the remembrance dear.*

[All's Well That Ends Well V iii 19]

Reinforce it with a tiresome cliché
> *What damned error but some sober brow will bless it*
> *And approve it with a text,*
> *Hiding the grossness with fair ornament.*

[The Merchant of Venice III ii 78]

Concede a short putt being assured of a greater bounty
> *Springes to catch woodcocks.*

[Hamlet I iii 115]

Counterfeit bonhomie
> *That one may smile and smile and be a villain.*

[Hamlet I v 108]

> *There's daggers in men's smiles.*

[Macbeth II iii 146]

Be ready with misleading advice
> *They'll take suggestion as a cat laps milk*

[The Tempest II i 279]

And the 'carelessly' dropped nugget of wisdom
> *Ill deeds are doubled with an evil word.*

[Comedy of Errors III ii 2]

A risky ploy to develop
> *That glib and oily art*
> *To speak and purpose not.*

[King Lear I i 225]

The best laid schemes

> *Now let it work; mischief thou art afoot.*
> *Take thou what course thou wilt.*

[Julius Caear III ii 265]

But beware lurking nemesis

> *It is the bright day that brings forth the adder*
> *And that craves wary walking.*

[Julius Caesar II i 18]

> *For 'tis the sport to have the engineer*
> *Hoist with his own petard.*

[Hamlet III iv 207]

Chapter 4: The First Tee.

Getting the first drive away in reasonable shape, is a matter of paramount concern to most golfers-It assumes an importance far and away greater than any other shot in the round. There you are, in full view of the clubhouse, with all those piercing eyes, critically fixed on every millimeter of your back swing; it's enough to make even the grooviest of swings wobble. Moreover, it sets the tone for the rest of the round. A modest one hundred and fifty yards down the middle and you're set fair : screw it up and the brain cells never stop jangling. Some appear to ride the situation with serene confidence while those of inferior mettle either freeze or exhibit the nervous tremblings of the blancmange, all suffused in a red mist. WS awaits.

The fateful summons:- On the tee
> *It is a knell that summons thee to heaven,*
> *Or to hell.*

[Macbeth II i 62]

An uncivil invitation to get started
> *Will you shog off?*

[Henry V II i 43]

Addressing the ball
> *Farewell!*
> *God knows when we shall meet again.*

[Romeo and Juliet IV iii 14]

> *If we do meet again, why, we shall smile!*
> *If not, why then, this parting was well made.*

[Julius Caesar V i 118]

It could save all this hassle
> *O! that a man might know*
> *The end of this day's business ere it come.*

[Julius Caesar V i 123]

Indecision
> *Now I am cabbin'd, cribb'd, confin'd..*
> *Bound in to saucy doubts and fears.*

[Macbeth II i 62]

A last nervous check
> *Plucking the grass to see where sits the wind.*

[Merchant of Venice I i 18]

Transparent fear

> *His knees knocking*
> *And with a look so piteous in purport*
> *As if he had been loosed out of hell*
> *To speak of horrors.*

[Hamlet II i 79]

Baseless fancies

> *0 hateful error, melancholy's child*
> *Why dost thou show to the apt thoughts of men*
> *The things that are not.*

[Julius Caesar V iii 67]

Summoning up the blood

> *Now set the teeth and stretch the nostrils wide*
> *Hold hard the breath,*
> *And bend up every spirit to its full height.*

[Henry V III i 14]

Let's get on with it

> *If it were done when 'tis done*
> *Then 'twere well it were done quickly.*

[Macbeth I vii 58]

Still not sure

> *You look pale and gaze and put on fear*
> *And cast yourself in wonder.*

[Julius Caesar I iii 59]

I must not falter now!

> *Hold. Hold, my heart!*
> *And you my sinews, grow not instant old,*
> *But bear me stiffly up.*

[Hamlet I v 93]

Think of England!

> *And gentlemen in England now abed*
> *Shall think themselves accursed they were not here.*

[Henry V IV ii 63]

Trust in god

> *He that hath the steerage of my course direct my sail.*

[Romeo and Juliet I iv 113]

And cross your fingers

> *Whistle her off and let her down the wind.*

[Othello III iii 266]

Chapter 5: Strokes; the good, bad, and the ugly

Given that it is easier to dispatch a golf ball more cleanly from a tee peg than from a worm's eye view why is it that the subsequent shot ends up being played from impossible places? The inescapable truth is that there is no simple answer. The perfect swing with the wrong club is capable of producing horrors as dire as the right club in the hands of a gangling birdbrain. And what about those other imponderables? The mind in turmoil, or a passing thought at the top of the swing, and waywardness is the very best you can expect, disaster the more likely outcome.

W.S. bears witness.

Watch out for some real screamers
> *Contagious blastments are most imminent.*

[Hamlet I iii 42]

Another miscalculation
> *Where the flight so runs against all reason.*

[Macbeth II iv 13]

You'd never credit it
> *Before my god, I might not this believe*
> *Without the sensible and true avouch of mine own eyes.*

[Hamlet I i 56]

Macabre!
> *As from your graves rise up and walk like sprites*
> *To countenance this horror.*

[Macbeth II iii 77]

Really weird
> *Is this not something more than fantasy?*

[Hamlet I i 53]

Indescribable
> *O horror, horror, horror.*
> *Tongue nor heart*
> *Cannot conceive nor name thee.*

[Macbeth II iii 61]

Unbelievably wretched
> *'Twas strange 'twas passing strange,*
> *'Twas pitiful, 'twas wondrous pitiful.*

[Othello I iii 15]

A simple par three
What needed then that terrible dispatch?

[King Lear I ii 32]

No way to treat a brand new Titleist
This was the most unkindest cut of all..

[Julius Caesar III ii 180]

I dislike this sledge hammer grip of yours
We do it wrong being so majestical
To offer it this show of violence.

[Hamlet I i 143]

Bravado
I'll set my teeth,
And send to darkness all that stop me.

[Antony and Cleopatra III xiii 121]

A controlled draw might serve you better
My bonded hook
Shall pierce their slimy jaws.

[Antony and Cleopatra II v 12]

The air shot
Things in motion sooner catch the eye
Than what stirs not.

[Troilus and Cressida III iii 183]

Some divot
A huge half moon, a monstrous cantle out.

[Henry IV Pt.1 III i 99]

The coup-de-grace
This blow might be the be all
And the end all here.

[Macbeth I vii 1]

An eagle at the 18th will encourage you back again
The daintiest last
To make the end most sweet

[Richard II I iii 81]

Chapter 6: Shots; brave and cautious

The long handicapper is renowned for fantasising in the following way. If I hit my Sunday best I'm on the green for two, putting for an eagle, at worst a birdie. So, no holds barred, go for it! Reality intervenes, making a direct hit between the eyes, and another double bogie bites the dust. The alternative scenario sees discretion overcoming valour, and the percentage seems the better option. And the result of these tortuous thought processes - A succession of laboured shots stagger waywardly in the general direction of the hole to record, guess what? another double bogie.

To be bold or careful? Suit yourselves; the slings and arrows will outrage you either way - a well known morsel of Shakespearian philosophy.

The dilemma.

> *I am at war 'twixt will and will not.*

[Measure For Measure II ii 29]

The shame.

> *Wouldst thou have that*
> *Which thou esteem'st the ornament of life,*
> *And live a coward in thine own esteem,*
> *Letting 'I dare not' wait upon 'I would'?*

[Macbeth I vii 40]

Positive encouragement

> *Be bloody, bold and resolute.*

[Macbeth IV i 79]

Possible reward

> *Out of this nettle danger*
> *We pluck this flower safety.*

[Henry IV Pt1 II iii 2]

It's a lottery

> *Men that hazard all*
> *Do it in the hope of fair advantages.*

[Merchant of Venice II vii 18]

Then there's the rest of us

> *Be not afraid of greatness.*
> *Some men are born great,*
> *Some achieve greatness,*
> *And some have greatness thrust upon 'em.*

[Twelfth Night II v 138]

Once is enough

> *Cowards die many times before their deaths*
> *The valiant never taste of death but once.*

[Julius Caesar II ii 30]

So let's go for it

> *Boldness be my friend. Arm me audacity.*

[Cymbeline III iii 35]

All guns blazing

> *Disdaining fortune with his brandish'd steel*
> *Which smoked with bloody execution.*

[Macbeth I ii 6]

He cannot be serious!

> *Why, this is very midsummer madness.*

[Twelfth Night III iv 62]

Steady on!

> *And in thy best consideration*
> *Check this hideous rashness.*

[King Lear I i 150]

Listen to reason

> *It is too rash, too unadvised, too sudden,*
> *Too like the lightning,*
> *That hath ceased to be,*
> *Ere one can say it lightens.*

[Romeo And Juliet II ii 1]

I might have taken on too much here

> *It strains me past the compass of my wits.*

[Romeo and Juliet IV i 46]

Pace yourself

> *His rash fierce blaze of riot cannot last*
> *For violent fires soon burn out themselves.*
> *Small showers last long,*
> *But sudden storms are short.*

[Richard II II i 33]

More cautious whispers

> *Though sometimes it shows greatness, courage, blood,*
> *Yet oftentimes it doth present harsh rage.*

[Henry 1V Pt.1 III i 179]

> *Be wary then. Best safety lies in fear.*

[Hamlet I iii 43]

Will you never learn?

O that way madness lies.Let me shun that
No more of that.

[King Lear III iv 21].

On the other hand

Be not too tame neither,
But let discretion be your tutor.

[Hamlet III ii 16]

Don't blame me!

Condemn the fault
And not the actor of it.

[Measure for Measure II ii 37]

Brawn versus brain

O it is excellent to have a giant's strength,
But it is tyrannous to use it like a giant.

[Measure For Measure II i 107]

I'll live with my own folly

Why tell you me of moderation
The grief is fine.

[Troilus And Cressida IV iv 2]

Costly prudence

They lose it that buy it with much care.

[Merchant Of Venice I i 75]

Spare me the logic

O reason not the need.

[King Lear II iv 263]

Doing what comes naturally

Instinct is a great matter.
I was a coward on instinct.

[Henry IV Pt.1 II iv 304]

Revisionary thoughts

When our actions do not,
Our fears do make us traitors.

[Macbeth IV ii 3]

No nearer to resolution

So far hath discretion fought with nature.

[Hamlet I ii 4]

Get real!

I pray you, being weak, seem so.

[King Lear I iv 189]

Chapter 7: The End Game

Eighteen holes of ecstatic fulfilment. A round of unalloyed joy. A transport of delight to be recounted blow by blow to receptive listeners down the years. What a travesty of reality does that represent for all but a very select band. Should any of the eighteen holes come close to matching such fantasy you could dine out on it indefinitely.

The real world would be more closely represented by a woeful sequence ranging from the minor mishap to the downright disaster. The golfer leaving the last green, despondent and desperate might be forgiven for vowing to dispatch his instruments of terror to waste disposal ,never again to revisit that erstwhile theatre of dreams.

As always W.S. has shared your trauma, so who better to turn to for enlightenment and understanding.

Blessed relief

When the hurlyburly's done,
When the battle's lost and won.

[Macbeth I i 3]

That's all one.
Our play is done.

[Twelfth Night V i 393]

My bones would rest
That have but laboured to attain this hour.

[Julius Caesar V v 41]

The long day's task is done
And we must sleep.

[Antony and Cleopatra IV xii 35]

Philosophic acceptance

What's done and what's past help,
Should be past grief.

[The Winter's Tale III ii 223]

Things past redress
Are now with me past care.

[Richard II II iii 171]

Things at the worst will cease
Or else climb upward.

[Macbeth I ii 24]

The score card tells all
> *Sent to my account,*
> *With all my imperfections on my head.*

[Hamlet I v 78]

This could improve my chances
> *O God of battles, take from them now*
> *The sense of reckoning.*

[Antony and Cleopatra I i 14]

Physiological retribution
> *For this be sure*
> *To night thou shalt have cramps.*

[The Tempest I ii 323]

> *Not dead, not yet quite dead.*

[Othello V ii 88]

> *His flawed heart, alack too weak the conflict to support,*
> *Twixt two extremes of passion, joy and grief,*
> *Burst smilingly.*

[King Lear V iii 197]

Suicidal despair
> *This world I do renounce and in your sight*
> *Shake patiently my great affliction off.*

[King Lear IV vi 35]

> *My dismal scene I needs must act alone.*

[Romeo and Juliet IV iii 19]

As time goes by
> *The end crowns all,*
> *And that old common arbitrator, time,*
> *Will one day end it.*

[Troilus and Cressida IV v 223]

Coming to terms
> *Men must endure their going hence,*
> *Even as their coming hither.*
> *Ripeness is all.*

[King Lear V ii 9]

Doomsday is near.
> *Die all, die merrily.*

[Henry IV Pt.I IV i 130]

Go quietly as your lot ordains
> *When beggars die there are no comets seen*
> *The heavens themselves blaze forth the death of princes.*

[Julius Caesar II ii 30]

Chapter 8: The Nineteenth

It is common belief among golfers of a heightened clubable disposition that if the Nineteenth hole did not exist then neither would the other eighteen. The holders of this theory maintain firstly, that desolation shared is a misery halved; secondly, that a quick fix provided by the bar steward is the essential primer for blanking out the immediate past; and thirdly, that in sufficient quantity, this 'Lethe' water can transform a wretched round into one of promise and achievement-Why else, they say, would anyone want to come back for more! W.S. has the answers.

The promised land

> *This blessed plot, this other Eden,*
> *Demi-paradise.*

[Richard II II i 45]

All needs catered for

> *The death of each day's life' sore labor's bath,*
> *Balm of hurt minds,*
> *Great nature's second course.*
> *Chief nourisher in life's feast.*

[Macbeth II ii 36]

The long-sought stuff of dreams

> *How have I thought of this and these times*
> *I shall recount hereafter.*

[Julius Caesar I ii 164]

The spike bar, -first port of call

> *Now, whilst your purple hands do reek and smoke,*
> *Fulfil your pleasure.*

[Julius Caesar III i 159]

Liquid solace not enough

> *That comfort comes too late.*
> *'Tis like a pardon after execution.*

[Henry VIII IV ii 120]

Mutual gloom

> *Misery acquaints a man with strange bedfellows.*

[The Tempest II ii 38]

In this fantasy world of golfing anecdotes

> *We are arrant knaves all.*
> *Believe none of us.*

[Hamlet III i 84]

Never let the truth spoil a good story
> *We are such stuff as dreams are made on.*
>
> [The Tempest IV I 56]

Add a touch of colour
> *Filling their hearers with strange invention.*
>
> [Macbeth II iii 132]

Bad rounds make the best stories
> *The nature of bad news infects the teller.*
>
> [Antony and Cleopatra I ii 103]

Hard to bear
> *List a brief tale; And when told,*
> *O that my heart would burst!*
>
> [King Lear V iii 182]

However much it hurts
> *Draw thy breath in pain to tell my story.*
>
> [Hamlet V ii 340]

Tell it, warts and all!
> *I will a plain unvarnished tale deliver.*
>
> [Othello I iii 135]

You'll not believe this
> *Sit down awhile, and let us once again assail your ears,*
> *That are so fortified against our story.*
>
> [Hamlet I i 30]

> *I could a tale unfold whose lightest word*
> *Would harrow up thy soul, freeze thy young blood,*
> *Make thy two eyes, like stars, start from their spheres,*
> *Thy knotted locks to part,*
> *And each particular hair to stand on end*
> *Like quills upon the fretful porpentine.*
>
> [Hamlet I v 13]

The real truth
> *A mingled yarn, good and ill together:*
> *Our virtues would be proud if our faults whipped them not;*
> *And our crimes would despair*
> *If we were not cherished by our own virtues.*
>
> [All's Well That Ends Well IV iii 66]

Faithfully recorded and garnished with age
> *Old men forget; yet all shall be forgot,*
> *But he'll remember with advantages*
> *What feats he did that day.*
>
> [Henry V IV iii 49]

Recall unaffected by wine

> Then shall our names,
> Familiar in his mouth as household words,
> Be in their flowing cups freshly remembered

[Henry V IV iii 51]

We don't hold with this

> An honest tale speeds best
> Being plainly told.

[Richard III IV iv 357]

Every detail

> Who loses, who wins; who's in, who's out
> And take upon us the mystery of things

[King Lear V iii 14]

Yarns of yester-year

> So we'll live and pray and sing
> And tell old tales,
> And laugh at gilded butterflies.

[King Lear V iii 12]

To be passed on

> This story shall the good man teach his son;
> And Crispin Crispian
> Shall ne'er go by
> From this day
> To the ending of the world
> But we in it shall be remembered

[Henry V IV iii 56]

Even the worst games evoke a perverse nostalgia

> Wherein I spoke
> Of most disastrous chances
> Of moving accidents,
> By flood and field.

[Othello I iii 128]

A good story is timeless

> How many ages hence
> Shall this our lofty scene be acted o'er?

[Julius Caesar III i 11]

A final confession

> *I like this place*
> *And willingly could spend my time in it.*

[As You Like It II iv 89]

Chapter 9: Putting

Putting they say, is an art all of its own, as if it had nothing to do with the game of golf at all. Many wish it hadn't, particularly those afflicted with the 'yips' and other chronic maladies. And yes, they have a point don't they? The putting surface, except that it's covered in grass, bears little resemblance to the rest of the course. You would think, with its beautifully manicured cut, that it would present far fewer problems than the rest. There is a further major difference however. Elsewhere there are acres of space for the ball to come to rest, and comparatively speaking, it's of little consequence where. Conversely, the green has a four and a quarter inch diameter target,- and there's the rub!- so many pitfalls, with slopes and borrows conspiring to give eye and brain a real pasting. W.S. muses.

Desirable qualities

Blessed are those whose blood and judgement
Are so well commingled.

[Hamlet III ii 67]

Not a pretty sight

His gashed stabs looked like
A breach in nature.

[Macbeth II iii 112]

Inflated confidence

'Tis not so deep as a well,
Nor so wide as a church door,
But 'tis enough, 'twill serve.

[Romeo and Juliet III i 93]

Reading the line

Bias and thwart. not answering the aim.

[Troilus and Cressida I ii 15]

Mixed messages

Oft the eye deceives, the mind being troubled.

[Venus and Adonis 1068]

The error of our eye directs our mind,
Minds sway'd by eyes are full of turpitude.

[Troilus and Cressida III ii 45]

Not always clear!

But canst thou guess that he doth aim at it?

[Richard III III ii 44]

Seeing is not always believing

> *When the devout religion of mine eye*
> *Maintains such falsehood.*

[Romeo and Juliet I ii 88]

The vital putt paralysis

> *I have a faint cold fear thrills through my veins*
> *That almost freezes up the heat of life.*

[Romeo And Juliet IV iii 14]

The silent prayer

> *Hold, hold my heart; And you my sinews,*
> *Grow not instant old, but bear me stiffly up.*

[Hamlet I v 93]

The long putt hangs over the lip

> *Give sorrows words*
> *The grief that does not speak*
> *Whispers the o'er fraught heart*
> *And bids it break.*

[Macbeth IV iii 208]

And still it'll not drop

> *His brains still beating puts him thus*
> *From fashion of himself.*

[Hamlet III i 173]

I cannot believe it

> *You do look, my son, in a mov'd sort,*
> *As if you were dismay'd.*

[The Tempest IV i 146]

The anguished cry of a vanished hope

> *At last, he raised a sigh so piteous and profound*
> *That it did seem to shatter all his bulk,*
> *And end his being.*

[Hamlet II i 94]

Missing the unmissable

> *I am afraid to think what I have done*
> *Look on' t again, I dare not.*

[Macbeth II ii 50]

Curses!

> *My words fly up my thoughts remain below*
> *Words without thoughts never to heaven go.*

[Hamlet III iii 97]

The red mist returns

>The body's delicate,
>The tempest in my mind doth from my senses
>Take all feeling else.

[King Lear III iv 12]

The damned cup

>Curs'd be the hand that made these fatal holes!
>Curs'd be the heart that had the heart to do it!

[Richard III I ii 14]

I despise thee!

>Thou detestable maw
>Thou womb of death.

[Romeo and Juliet V iii 45]

I'm comin' to getcha!

>Tremble thou wretch, that hast within thee
>Undivulged crimes unwhipp'd of justice!.

[King Lear III ii 51]

Ball rims the hole, gathering speed

>And then it started like a guilty thing
>Upon a fearful summons.

[Hamlet I i 148]

In! - and out again.

>Let me not burst in ignorance but tell,
>Why the sepulchre wherein we saw thee quietly enurn'd
>Hath op'd his ponderous jaws,
>To cast thee up again.

[Hamlet I iv 46]

A man can take just so much!

>Unfriended, new adapted to our hate
>Dowered with our curse
>And strangered with our oath.

[King Lear I i 203]

The end is nigh

>The extravagant and erring spirit
>Hies to his confine.

[Hamlet I i 154]

A triumphal end

>Down, down to hell
>And say I sent thee thither!

[King Henry VI Pt. III V vi 67]

Buried at last

      Rest, rest perturbed spirit!

                                   [Hamlet I v 182]

Chapter 10: Golf Club Characters

The Golf Club - A microcosm of the world at large-Or so you might think. Not a bit of it! As an association it can throw up more 'characters' to the square yard than you can wave a Complete Works Of Shakespeare at. W.S. himself was left in wonder at its infinite variety. '0 brave new world that has such people in't' (The Tempest)

Divers raconteurs

> *A fellow of infinite jest,*
> *Of most excellent fancy.*

[Hamlet V i 180]

> *A gentleman that loves to hear himself talk*
> *And will speak more in a minute*
> *Than he will stand to in a month.*

[Romeo And Juliet II iv 143]

> *He draweth out the thread of his verbosity*
> *Finer than the staple of his argument.*

[Love's Labour's Lost V i 15]

Wisecracker

> *This fellow 's wise enough to play the fool.*
> *And to do that well craves a kind of wit.*

[Twelfth Night III i 56]

> *Better a witty fool than a foolish wit.*

[Twelfth Night I v 33]

Here it comes.

> *Look, he's winding up the watch of his wit;*
> *By and by it will strike.*

[Tempest II i 12]

The Club bore

> *0 he is as tedious as a tired horse.*
> *Worse than a smokey house.*

[Henry IV Pt.I III i 158]

> *He speaks an infinite deal of nothing.*

[Merchant Of Venice I i 114]

> *I had rather live with cheese and garlic*
> *In a windmill far,*
> *Than have him talk to me*
> *In any house in Christendom.*

[Henry IV Pt.I III i 161]

More empty vessels

> *He was but as the cuckoo is in June,*
> *Heard, but not regarded.*

[Henry IV Pt.I III ii 75]

Tolerance gives way to banishment

> *Let the doors be shut upon him,*
> *That he may play the fool nowhere*
> *But in's own house.*

[Hamlet III i 132]

Captains various

> *Some are born great, some achieve greatness,*
> *And some have greatness thrust upon 'em.*

[Twelfth Night II v 130]

Captain titanic

> *Why, man, he doth bestride the narrow world*
> *Like a colossus,*
> *And we petty men walk under his huge legs*
> *And peep about*
> *To find ourselves dishonourable   graves.*

[Julius Caesar I ii 134]

Captain pretentious

> *Dressed in a little brief authority,*
> *Most ignorant of what he's most assured.*

[Measure for Measure II ii 117]

Captain aloof

> *Looks in the clouds, scorning the base degrees*
> *By which he did ascend.*

[Julius Caesar I iii 23]

Captain compromise

> *Lofty and sour to those that loved him not,*
> *But to those men that sought him*
> *Sweet as summer.*

[Henry VIII IV ii 53]

One in a million

> *He was a man, take him for all in all*
> *We shall not look upon his like again.*

[Hamlet I ii 187]

The golfer's Jack the lad

> *For he is given to sports, wildness*
> *And much company.*

[Julius Caesar II i 189]

Acknowledging a foible or two

> *Wine I loved deeply, dice dearly;*
> *And in woman out-paramour'd the Turk.*

[King Lear III iv 90]

Indispensable member

> *Banish plump Jack and banish all the world.*

[Henry IV Pt. I II iv 520]

The dedicated wino

> *I am known to be one that loves a cup of hot wine,*
> *With not a drop of alloying Tiber in' t.*

[Corialanus II i 52]

Strong, silent golfers

> *I do know of these that only are reputed wise*
> *For saying nothing.*

[The Merchant Of Venice I i 96]

And the seriously down-in the mouth

> *And other of such vinegar aspect*
> *That they'll not show their teeth in way of smile.*

[The Merchant Of Venice I i 53]

The Club analyst

> *He is a great observer, and he looks*
> *Quite through the deeds of men.*

[Julius Caesar I ii 202]

The Club know-all

> *Dressed in an opinion of wisdom, gravity*
> *And profound conceit.*

[The Merchant Of Venice I i 92]

The Club creep

> *He does smile his face into more lines*
> *Than are in the new map,*
> *With the augmentation of the Indies.*

[Twelfth Night III ii 85]

> *Nature hath fram'd strange fellows in her time,*
> *Some that will evermore peep through their eyes,*
> *And laugh like parrots at a bagpiper.*

[The Merchant Of Venice I i 52]

The loner

> *I know a man*
> *Who had this trick of melancholy.*

[All's Well That Ends Well III ii 8]

It hurts when I laugh

> *Seldom he smiles, and smiles in such a sort*
> *As if he mock'd himself*
> *And scorn'd his spirit, that could be mov'd*
> *To smile at anything.*

[Julius Caesar I ii 20]

His critical analysis of your swing can damage your health

> *He thinks too much,*
> *Such men are dangerous.*

[Julius Caesar I ii 194]

The insatiable, 'must have the latest cure all' golfers

> *No sooner knew the reason*
> *But they sought the remedy.*

[As you Like It V ii 34]

The social member

> *I, that am not shap'd for sportive tricks.*

[King Richard III I i 14]

Try it. The exercise will do you good.

> *Will he not upon our fair request untent his person*
> *And share the air with us?*

[Troilus and Cressida II iii 162]

Another excuse

> *I am not gamesome.*
> *I do lack some part of that quick spirit.*

[Julius Caesar I ii 28]

Try a basin full of this guy- he'll cheer you up!

> *A trusty villain, sir, that very oft'*
> *When I am dull with care and melancholy,*
> *Lightens my humour with his merry jests.*

[The Comedy of Errors I ii 23]

The Golf Club- a social leveller

> *Since every Jack became a gentleman*
> *There's many a gentle person made a Jack.*

[King Richard III I i 72]

Chapter 11: Etiquette

As an item for legislation you might think that etiquette in golf would hardly reach first base. After all, to the lady or gentleman golfer its tenets are inborn, natural, instinctive. Whoever witnessed players of such sensitivity falling short on such matters as, "Consideration for other players", or "Care of the course." Nor is it conceivable that they would default over the replacement of divots, raking bunkers or repairing pitch marks. The fact that these basic courtesies are mentioned at all in the Rules of Golf can only be interpreted as pointed reminders to those middle class, Johnny-come-lately types who have infiltrated a former, blue blooded and exclusive preserve. Professionalism too has something to answer for; or why is it bruited about that a nineteenth century professional at Walton Heath (or so the story goes) felt constrained never to enter the clubhouse by the front door? It is significant too, that the first thirteen Articles and Laws were drawn up by the "Gentlemen" of Leith, without even a mention, you can bet, of 'Etiquette'. So, what did the impeccable W.S. make of it all?

Unseemly behaviour

> *There have been players that I have seen play,*
> *That, have so strutted and bellowed*
> *That I have thought that nature's journeymen had made men,*
> *And not made them well,*
> *They imitated humanity so abominably.*

[Hamlet III ii 19]

By contrast

> *We knew not the doctrine of ill-doing,*
> *No, nor dreamed that any did.*

[The Winter's Tale I ii 70]

But I admit

> *For my own part, I may speak it to my shame*
> *I have a truant been to chivalry.*

[Henry IV Pt. I V i 100]

Reproof from on high

> *Is there no respect of place, persons,*
> *Nor time in you?*

[Twelfth Night II iii 101]

But don't over react

> *O'er step not the modesty of nature,*
> *For anything so overdone*
> *Is from the purpose of playing.*

[Hamlet III ii 19]

Unpardonable sins

> *The common curse of mankind,*
> *Folly and ignorance*

[Troilus and Cressida II iii 26]

Not in front of the ladies

> *Mend your speech a little,*
> *Lest you may mar your fortunes.*

[King Lear I i 93]

Slow play

> *Stand not upon the order of your going,*
> *But go at once.*

[Macbeth III iv 119]

Don't stand about

> *Taste your legs ,sir; put them to motion.*

[Twelfth Night III I 75]

A painful reproof

> *How now!*
> *Which of your hips has the most profound sciatica?*

[Measure For Measure I ii 56]

You cannot go faster than that

> *I have speeded hither*
> *With the very extremist inch of possibility.*

[Henry IV PtII IV iii 32]

Slow play vindicated

> *Too swift arrives as tardy as too slow.*

[Romeo And Juliet II vi 15]

An even pace is better

> *He tires betimes that spurs too fast betimes.*

[Richard II II i 36]

There can be other priorities

> *Our haste from hence*
> *Is of so quick condition,*
> *That it prefers itself*
> *And leaves unquestion'd*
> *Matters of needful value.*

[Measure for Measure I i 54]

Come off it

> *The excuse that thou dost make*
> *In this delay*
> *Is longer than the tale,*
> *Thou dost excuse.*

[Romeo and Juliet II v 38]

Laid back ripostes

> *Tis the breathing time of day with me.*

[Hamlet V ii 168]

> *The spirit of the time shall teach me speed.*

[King John IV ii 176]

And furthermore

> *Do you not see that I am out of breath?*

[Romeo and Juliet II v 36]

Better late than never

> *Finding ourselves too slow,*
> *We put on a compelled vigour.*

[Hamlet IV vi 17]

Finally giving way with due courtesy

> *Sweep on you fat and greasy citizens.*

[As You Like It II i 55]

The involuntary divot

> *O, pardon me, thou bleeding piece of earth !*

[Julius Caesar III i 254]

An even bigger divot

> *A huge half moon*
> *A monstrous cantle out.*

[Henry IV Pt.I III i 97]

Repairing divots

> *Though I am a native here,*
> *And to the manner born,*
> *It is a custom more honour'd in the breach,*
> *Than the observance.*

[Hamlet I iv 14]

Improving the lie of the ball

> *We took this mattock,*
> *And this spade from him.*

[Romeo and Juliet V iii 184]

End of game courtesies duly dispatched

> *Ne'er shook hands nor bade farewell to him,*
> *Till he unseam'd him from the nave to the chaps,*
> *And fixed his head upon our battlements.*

[Macbeth I i 21]

Chapter 12: Abuse, and other homespun discourtesies.

It is difficult to believe in these days of liberal free speech, and the disrespectful outpourings against society's pillars of rectitude, that the society of Shakespeare's acquaintance could outrival the crudest practitioners of to-day. And should it be thought that the golf courses of sixteenth century Stratford and St. Andrews were immune from such rustic vulgarity, stand by for a barrage of evidence from your very own eye-witness, W.S.

The Scottish curse
> *A south-west blow on ye, and blister ye all o'er.*
>
> [The Tempest I iii 323]

Harmless fellow golfer, still in shock
> *Thou cream-faced loon!*
> *Where got'st thou that goose look?*
>
> [Macbeth V iii 2]

Opponent takes a winning lead
> *Thou art a boil,*
> *A plague- sore, an embossed carbuncle,*
> *In my corrupted blood..*
>
> [King Lear II iv 222]

Partner misses easy putt
> *Thou debosh'd fish thou!*
>
> [The Tempest III ii 30]

Please be quiet
> *What bloody man is that?*
>
> [Macbeth I ii 1]

Succinct exasperation
> *Out dunghill!*
>
> [King Lear IV vi 240]

Not best pleased with partner's anaemic play
> *If he were open'd and you find so much blood in his liver*
> *As will clog the foot of a flea,*
> *I'll eat the rest of th'anatomy.*
>
> [Twelfth Night III ii 58]

Getting really personal
> *Away thou issue of a mangy dog.*
>
> [Timon of Athens IV ii 3]

Ladies, please!
> *You witch, you hag, you baggage,*
> *You polecat, you ronyon!*

[Merry Wives of Windsor IV ii 162]

Please try to calm down
> *These are but wild and whirling words .*

[Hamlet I v 133]

Even royal persons get the treatment
> *Go hang thyself*
> *In thine own heir- apparent garters.*

[Henry IV Pt. I II ii 42]

Be reasonable
> *It is not meet that every nice offence*
> *Should bear this comment.*

[Julius Caesar IV iii 6]

Get lost!
> *Go to, I'll no more on't, it hath made me mad.*

[Hamlet III ii 145]

O.K If that's the way you want it
> *Thou clay-brain'd guts,*
> *Thou knotty-pated fool,*
> *Thou whoreson, obscene, greasy tallow- catch.*

[Henry IV Pt. I II iv 220]

You can have it. – With knobs on.
> *A knave, a rascal, an eater of broken meats*
> *A base, proud, shallow, beggarly, three suited,*
> *Hundred pound, filthy, worsted-stocking knave.*

[King Lear I ii 13]

Tit for tat
> *A plague upon your epileptic visage.*

[King Lear I ii 76]

> *Thou drone, thou snail, thou slug, thou sot.*

[Comedy of Errors II ii 196]

> *You whoreson callionly barber-monger.*

[King Lear II ii 29]

Women!
> *Get thee to a nunnery, go, farewell!*

[Hamlet III ii 136]

> *Go thy ways, wench; serve God!*

[Romeo and Juliet II v 44]

Chapter 13: Hanging Fire

To see some golfers standing over the ball preparatory to actually playing it you might think that the ball had induced a hypnotic trance from which no outside influence could rouse them. Have they forgotten what they were there for, you wonder. What thought processes are afoot? And should this pantomime be played out on the green as well as the tee, the waiting is almost beyond endurance. A crucial putt and you could be there forever! But you have to sympathise. In varying degrees we have all suffered the mental turmoil of a thousand conflicting thoughts, and hoping that the emerging one will lead to actually hitting the ball, somewhere, anywhere! And what about those noises off? real or imaginary. W.S. was particularly susceptible to such distractions.

It's all in the mind

> *There is nothing either good or bad*
> *But thinking makes it so.*

[Hamlet II ii 248]

Get on with it

> *And thus the native hue of resolution is sicklied o'er*
> *With the pale cast of thought,*
> *And enterprises of great pith and moment,*
> *With this regard, their currents turn awry,*
> *And lose the name of action.*

[Hamlet III i 84]

This could cost us the match

> *Our doubts are traitors,*
> *And make us lose the good we oft might win*
> *By fearing to attempt.*

[Measure for Measure I iv 78]

A blue funk

> *Between the acting of a dreadful thing*
> *And the first motion,*
> *All the interim is like a phantasma*
> *Or a hideous dream.*

[Julius Caesar I i 63]

How much longer?

> *While one with moderate haste*
> *Might tell a hundred.*

[Hamlet I ii 237]

51

Minor irritations

> *A mote it is to trouble the mind's eye.*

[Hamlet I i 112]

The brain cells are at war again

> *So full of shapes is fancy*
> *That it alone is high fantastical.*

[Twelfth Night I i 14]

> *A man into whom nature hath so crowded humours*
> *That his valour is crushed into folly,*
> *His folly sauced with discretion.*

[Troilus and Cressida I ii 22]

Becoming obsessive

> *Whence is that knocking?*
> *How is't with me, when every noise appalls me?*

[Macbeth II ii 55]

Leading to sheer dread

> *Distilled, almost to jelly with the act of fear.*

[Hamlet I ii 205]

Still abstracted by the last miss?

> *To mourn a mischief that is past and gone*
> *Is the next way to draw new mischief on.*

[Othello I iii 204]

Forget it

> *Let us not burden our remembrances*
> *With a heaviness that's gone.*

[The Tempest V i 198]

Let's go beat the hell out of 'em

> *On lusty gentlemen!*

[Romeo and Juliet I iv 113]

Chapter 14: Dress

Those of us who never had the privilege of seeing Old Tom Morris in action have to make do with photographs of this legendary golfer. Mention is made here only to contrast the golfing attire worn by him and his contemporaries with that sported by professionals and their followers of today. Gone are the collars and ties and, if the photographs do not lie, the waistcoat and tweed jacket as well. But may-be golf club officialdom nowadays has got the dress code all the wrong way round and the collar and tie really is for the course, not indoors!

W.S. of course preceded Old Tom by a decade or two and was not slow to comment on some of the on-course sights of his day.

Incredible attire

> *There's two or three of us have seen strange sights.*

[Julius Caesar I iii 138]

Spare us the Tartan plaids

> *What are these, so withered and so wild*
> *In their attire?*

[Macbeth I iii 39]

And the knee-length hose.

> *Ha ha, he wears cruel garters.*

[King Lear II iv 6]

And the ostentation

> *Who commended thy yellow stockings*
> *And wished to see thee cross- gartered?*

[Twelfth Night II v 135]

The sartorial europhile

> *I think he bought his doublet in Italy,*
> *His round hose in France, his bonnet in Germany*
> *And his behaviour everywhere.*

[Merchant of Venice I ii 78]

Casual indifference to the dress code

> *His stockings fouled, ungartered and down-gyved to his ankle*

[Hamlet II i 79]

Time for reappraisal

> *His youthful hose, well-saved,*
> *A world too wide for his shrunk shank*

[As You Like It II vii 1]

Pro's shop talk
> *Look what a wardrobe here is for thee!*

[The Tempest IV i 222]

Push the boat out
> *Costly be thy habit as thy purse can buy*
> *Rich, not gaudy*
> *For th'apparel oft proclaims the man.*

[Hamlet I iii 72]

I've a good line in waterproofs
> *Thou wert better in thy grave*
> *Than to answer with thy uncover'd body*
> *The extremity of the skies.*

[King Lear III iv 100]

Reports from the course
> *Four rogues in buckram let drive at me.*

[Henry IV Pt.II II v 189]

Time to take cover
> *Three misbegotten knaves in Kendal green*
> *Came at my back and let drive at me.*

[Henry IV Pt.I II iv 2]

Quirky habits
> *Put your bonnet to its right use;*
> *'Tis for the head..*

[Hamlet II ii 92]

It'll never catch on
> *Why wearest thou that glove upon thy cap?*

[Henry V IV vii 1]

Sartorial vendetta
> *Let them come.*
> *They come like sacrifices in their trim,*
> *And to the fire-ey'd maid of smoky war*
> *All hot and bleeding will we offer them.*

[Henry I.Pt.1 1 i 112]

Black for all occasions
> *I have that which passes show*
> *These but the trappings and the suits of woe.*

[Hamlet I ii 76]

Chapter 15: The Rules Of Golf

As any schoolboy will tell you, there's only one thing to do with a rule, break it! And if the consequences of that are too dire, ignore it!

That allowed, the first 'Code of Conduct' drawn up by the regulators of the game in 1774 consisted not of Rules at all but of 'Articles and Laws'. Now, breaking the law has an awesome ring to it, with overtones of horrendous penalties. Rules on the other hand sound much more benign. So the administrators duly became much more accommodating, producing the 15 Rules of 1851. Over the years these have not only multiplied but have been subject to innumerable amendments and interpretations, culminating in the sophisticated bible we have to-day.

And that is fortunate for most of us. So numerous are they that you need to take early retirement to afford the leisure to read them, and so abstruse as to require a law degree to unravel the mysteries. So, except for a few know-all johnnies nobody bothers to read them. You can of course, airing your cursory knowledge use them to your own advantage. After all, they're not laws, merely rules, as W.S. would freely acknowledge.

The abridged version

> *Here are a few of the unpleasantest words*
> *That ever blotted paper!*

[Merchant of Venice. III 252]

Freely interpreted

> *Flout 'em and scout 'em and scout 'em and flout 'em*
> *Thought is free.*

[The Tempest. III ii 117]

The unabridged version

> *And now I will unclasp a secret book*
> *And to your quick conceiving discontents*
> *I'll read you matters deep and dangerous.*

[Henry IV Pt I I iii 188]

The hard back version

> *Was ever book containing such vile matter*
> *So fairly bound?*

[Romeo and Juliet III ii 91]

The Welsh version
> *Will you vouchsafe me, look you,*
> *As partly touching or concerning the disciplines.*

[Henry V III ii 88]

The 'who cares' version
> *For mine own part it was Greek to me.*

[Julius Caesar I ii 283]

A circumstance not covered by the rules
> *It would be argument for a week,*
> *Laughter for a month,*
> *And a good jest for ever.*

[Henry IV Pt.I II ii 91]

Referee intervenes to settle argument
> *Seal up the mouth of outrage for a while,*
> *Till we can clear these ambiguities.*

[Romeo and Juliet V iii 214]

Be sure you're in the right before seeking his ruling
> *Take heed, for he holds vengeance in his hands*
> *To hurl upon their heads that break his law.*

[Richard III I iv 184]

> *For, as thou urgest justice, be assured*
> *Thou shalt have justice.*
> *More than thou desirest.*

[Merchant Of Venice IV i 315]

The final reference
> *I do see the very book indeed*
> *Where all my sins are writ.*

[Richard II IV I 274]

The ultimate sanction
> *Arrest them to the answer of the law*
> *And god acquit them of their practices.*

[Henry V II ii 122]

Your putt or mine?
> *In the way of bargain*
> *I'll cavil on the ninth part of a hair.*

[Henry IV Pt.I II i 139]

That serious eh?
> *I will make a Star Chamber matter of it.*

[Merry Wives Of Windsor I i 1]

Bringing the riff raff to heel

> There is a law in each well ordered nation
> To curb those raging appetites
> That are most disobedient
> And refractory.

[Troilus and Cressida II ii 180]

Without deterring others

> We must not make a scarecow of the law.

[Measure or Measure II i 2]

Dismissive response

> The bloody book of law.

[Othello I iii 84]

Re writing the rules

> And never yet could frame my will to it,
> And therefore,
> Frame the law unto my will.

[Henry VI II iv 7]

Or bending them

> Bidding the law make curtsy to their will.

[Measure for Measure I iv 174]

 Or ignoring them

> The law hath not been dead
> Though it hath slept.

[Measure for Measure II ii 90]

Or adopting a selective policy

> So to enforce or qualify the laws
> As to your own self seems good.

[Measure For Measure I i 64]

> Thou conclud'st like the sanctimonious pirate
> That went to sea with the Ten Commandments
> But scrap'd one out of the table.

[Measure For Measure I ii 8]

But you flout them at your peril

> He hath resisted law
> And therefore,
> Law shall scorn him further trial

[Coriolanus   III I 268]

Honesty's the best policy then?

> Keep o' the windy side of the laws.

[Twelfth Night III iv 156]

Still bemused by the legal niceties

> *Zounds! I was never so bethumped with words*

[King John II i 266]

The final solution

> *The first thing we do,*
> *Let's kill all the lawyers.*

[Henry IV Pt.II IV ii 73]

Chapter 16: The Philosophisers

Golfers fall into two categories, each representing a distinctive approach to the game's ups and downs of fortune. One group is typified by the ranters and ravers, and the other by the calmly compliant. The former cry out to the heavens, appealing to the gods in a reproachful way as though they were the victims of a divine conspiracy. The degree of vehemence displayed is of course inversely proportional to their own inadequacy By contrast the philosophically minded accept what's on offer with serene resignation - a martyrdom leading some to suicidal dejection. W.S. had joined battle with them all.

There's a divinity which shapes our ends,
Rough-hew them how we will.

[Hamlet V ii 10]

What's gone and what's past help
Should be past grief.

[The Winter's Tale III ii 223]

Come what come may,
Time and the hour runs through the roughest day.

[Macbeth I iii 147]

Things without all remedy should be without regard.
What's done is done.

[Macbeth III ii 11]

The weight of this sad time we must obey,
Speak what we feel not what we ought to say.

[King Lear V iii 323]

What's past and what's to come is strewed with husks
And formless ruin of oblivion.

[Troilus And Cressida V v 165]

Wise men ne'er sit and wail their loss,
But cheerily seek how to redress their harms.

[Henry VI Pt.III V iv 2]

Let's not burden our remembrances
With a heaviness that's gone.

[The Tempest V i 198]

Great men great losses should endure.

[Julius Caesar IV iii 191]

A sad tale's best for winter.

[The Winter's Tale II i 24]

He robs himself that spends a bootless grief.

[Othello I iii 209]

Let me embrace thee sour adversity
For wise men say it is the wisest course.

[Henry VI Pt. III III i 24]

Chapter 17: Do you come here often?

How often have you heard fellow golfers, even on their own course exclaim "Well, I've never played a shot from here before"

Should you be playing in a Foursomes of course, it's a not too well disguised inference that your partner is a complete and utter clodpoll for engineering your current predicament. It's well known that he regularly indulges in these pioneering safaris but no one, as yet has dared to offer the appropriate advice.

Nor would it be wise to deal with him too harshly; you're just as likely, on occasions, to screw things up on your own account. Look at some of the nightmare situations that bedevilled W.S.

Wayward golfer rejoins the group

> *How now my headstrong,*
> *Where have you been gadding?*

[Romeo and Juliet IV ii 16]

Beyond the frontiers of darkness

> *The undiscovered country from whose bourn*
> *No traveller returns.*

[Hamlet III i 79]

A smouldering search

> *What art thou*
> *That dost grumble there i'the straw.?*

[King Lear II iv 43]

That which means not to be found

> *Search every acre in the high-grown field*
> *And bring him to our eye.*

[King Lear IV i 7]

Blind panic

> *Is't lost? Is't gone?*
> *Speak, is't out o' the way?*

[Othello III iv 80]

Play a provisional ball

> *The self-same flight, the self-same way,*
> *With more advised watch,*
> *To find the other forth.*

[Merchant of Venice I i 141]

A stupefying situation

His grief grew puissant
And the strings of life began to crack,
And there I left him, tranc'd.

[King Lear V iii 214]

Chapter 18: The Big Match

The build up of emotions in advance of an important event begins its feverish journey in an atmosphere of calm detachment. While the contest is still a distant prospect all is serene optimism which, at its peak, manifests itself in the drafting of a winner's acceptance speech. As zero hour approaches self-belief gives way progressively to doubt, cold feet and dread. Add the alternate displays of bravado and panic, toss in a smidgen of despair and you touch bottom with a gibbering idiot, teeing off in a blue funk, shrouded in a red mist.

On the other hand, all could be suffused in dynamic fervour; a bristling to be off and show 'em a thing or two. But lest we get too carried away ,such a scenario might possibly betray a precursory half hour at the bar, summoning up the blood.

No stranger to imbibing an anticipatory jar or two of Dutch courage, our Boer's Head regular W.S. had experienced the whole cauldron of emotions.

Eager anticipation

> *0, let the hours be short*
> *Till fields and blows and groans applaud our sport!.*

> [Henry IV Pt.I I iii 300]

Light hearted confidence

> *And all this day an unaccustomed spirit*
> *Lifts me above the ground with cheerful thoughts.*

> [Romeo and Juliet V i 3]

The waiting's over

> *Now all the youth of England are on fire*
> *And silken dalliance in the wardrobe lies.*

> [Henry V II i 1]

Just light the blue touch paper

> *0 for a Muse of fire that would ascend*
> *The brightest heaven of invention.*

> [Henry V Prologue]

Adrenalin's working overtime

> *Now could I drink hot blood*
> *And do such bitter business as the day*
> *Would quake to look on.*

> [Hamlet III ii 413]

Single-minded aim

> *I have no spur to prick the sides of my intent*
> *But only vaulting ambition.*

[Macbeth I vii 16]

Insatiable hunger

> *As if increase of appetite*
> *Had grown by what it fed on.*

[Hamlet I ii 143]

Inspirational encouragement

> *When the blast of war blows in our ears,*
> *Then imitate the action of the tiger:*
> *Stiffen the sinews, summon up the blood,*
> *Disguise fair nature with hard-favour'd rage.*

[Henry V II I i 5]

Look menacing

> *Come, stretch thy chest,*
> *And let thy eyes spout blood.*

[Troilus And Cressida V v 10]

The call to arms

> *Once more unto the breach, dear friends,*
> *Once more!*

[Henry V III i 1]

Final moments to countdown

> *He which hath no stomach for this fight*
> *Let him depart.*

[Henry V IV iii 35]

Impatient to be off

> *I see you stand like greyhounds in the slips,*
> *Straining upon the start.*

[Henry V III i 30]

> *Cry havoc and let slip the dogs of war!*

[Julius Caesar III i 270]

They're off!

> *The game's afoot:*
> *Follow your spirit and upon this charge*
> *Cry,' God for Harry, England, and St. George!'*

[Henry V III i 31]

Chapter 19: Body Language

Golfers mirror the rest of society. They come in all shapes and sizes, from the perfectly proportioned Adonis to those whose physical construction has been designed either by a committee or a faulty computer. (No attempt is made here to categorise female golfers) Unfair physical advantages abound-and it shows. For some, to engineer a swing that will come within a mile of the hitting area requires super-human effort; it's heart rending. However, given that some are more favourably endowed than others, let us also allow that body language is universal. The wry smile, the grimace, the gut-tearing, the cap in the air, the hurling of the club and other manifestations of ecstasy and dejection betray all alike. Yes, body language is a common language as W.S. testifies.

Deep concentration

And in thy face strange motions have appeared
Such as we see when men restrain their breath.

[Henry IV Pt.I II iii 57]

Deep despair

Ne'er pull your hat upon your brows;
Give sorrows words,
The grief that does not speak
Whispers the o'er fraught heart,
And bids it break.

[Macbeth IV iii 218]

Self-inflicted penance

Alas! Why gnaw you so your nether lip?

[Othello V ii 43]

A near miss

The windy suspiration of forced breath.

[Hamlet I ii 79]

Trudging dejection

'Tis like the forced gait
Of a shuffling nag.

[Henry IV Pt.I III i 35]

Ominous betrayal

By his face
Straight shall you know his heart.

[Richard III III iv 5]

Three putting can wear you down
The dejected 'haviour of the visage.

[Hamlet I ii 231]

Down the middle ball!
Thou hast a grim appearance
And thy face bears a command in it.

[Coriolanus IV v 66]

Vigorous back swing, feeble follow through
That strain again, it had a dying fall.

[Twelfth Night I i 4]

On the rack
His knees knocking,
And with a look so hideous in purport,
As if he had been loosed out of hell
To speak of horrors.

[Hamlet II i 8]

Urging the ball to bend by listing the trunk
'Tis very like he hath the falling sickness.

[Julius Caesar I ii 25]

Resigned to failure
A countenance more in sorrow than in anger.

[Hamlet I ii 23]

Is it all worth it ?
Is it not monstrous that this player here,
Tears in his eyes,
Distraction in's aspect, a broken voice,
And all for nothing!

[Hamlet II ii 544]

Chapter 20: A Man's Game

The macho image of golf has surely been consigned to history. The long-hitting ladies have long ago whammed such chauvinism way out of the ball park, progressively making inroads on an erstwhile male preserve. The story goes that years ago, at St. Andrews, they were restricted to a miniature ladies' course with a limit on the drive of eighty yards. Concessionary access otherwise was grudgingly allowed-'If they choose to play at times when the male golfers are feeding, or resting, no one can object'. It's doubtful if W.S. on the following evidence would have conceded so much.

So it is a man's game
> This is no world to play with mammets
> And to tilt with lips.
> We must have bloody noses and cracked crowns.
>
> [Henry 1V Pt.1 I iv 93]

No place for junior either
> To it Hal, Nay, you shall find no boy's play here,
> I can tell you!
>
> [Henry 1V Pt.1 V iv 75]

He'll not get far
> I have a man's mind, but a woman's might.
>
> [Julius Caesar II iv 6]

Cometh the hour
> O, the blood more stirs
> To rouse a lion than to start a hare!
>
> [Henry 1V Pt.1 I iii 197]

That's golf for you
> In the reproof of chance
> Lies the true proof of men.
>
> [Troilus and Cressida I ii 33]

Put your money where your mouth is
> Thy great employment will not bear question;
> Either say thou'lt do it,
> Or thrive by other means.
>
> [King Lear V iii 33]

Female preferences

> *Let me have men about me that are fat*
> *Sleek-headed men, and such as sleep o'nights.*

[Julius Caesar I ii 191]

Golf's more than just a game

> *A man cannot make him laugh*
> *But that's no marvel*
> *He drinks no wine.*

[Henry IV PtII IV iii 92]

Gender in doubt

> *God made him,*
> *And therefore let him pass for a man.*

[Merchant of Venice I ii 50]

Chapter 21: Links Courses

Traditionally favoured as venues for tough competitions like The Open, Links courses are by nature more formidable cookies to crack than the parkland versions of more recent origin. The former, carved out by God and nature, the latter designed by more earthly architects. As you would expect, it was the Links course, with its lunar like landscape that fell within the orbit of W.S. and his latter day sparring partners.

Not impressed
> *Uneven is the course I like it not.*

[Romeo and Juliet IV i 5]

What can you expect?
> *Diseased nature oftentimes breaks forth*
> *In strange eruptions;*
> *Oft' the teeming earth.*
> *Is with a kind of colic pinched and vexed.*

[Henry IV Pt I III i 2]

From reclaimed land
> *A thousand leagues of sea for an acre of barren ground*
> *Long heath, brown furze, anything.*

[The Tempest I i63]

Other typical features.
> *Rough quarries, rocks, and hills*
> *Whose heads touch heaven.*

[Othello I iii 14]

Not for the unwary
> *Congregated sands, traitors ensteep'd to clog the guileless.*

[Othello II i 69]

You should not mess about with nature
> *It was a great pity, so it was this villainous saltpetre*
> *Should be digged out of the bowels of the harmless earth.*

[Henry IV Pt.I I iii 57]

To make pot bunkers!
> *There's hell, there's darkness,*
> *There's the sulphurous pit;*
> *Burning, scalding stench.*

[King Lear IV vi 128]

Having a fatal attraction
> *The swallowing womb of this deep pit.*

[Titus Andronicus II iv 239]

Wherein lie further hazards
> *Descend to darkness*
> *And the burning lake.*

[Henry Vi Pt II I iv 75]

Scottish courses are not for the faint hearted
> *Safer shall he be upon the sandy plains*
> *Than where castles mounted stand.*

[Henry VIPt II I iv 70]

Compulsive torment
> *A stage where every man must play a part.*
> *And mine a sad one.*

[Merchant of Venice I i 98]

Chapter 22: The Caddie

As defined in the Rules of Golf; a Caddie is one who carries on handles a player's clubs during play and otherwise assists him in accordance with the Rules. Not to put too fine a point on it, he is the factotum of the golf course-the fetcher and carrier, butler, adviser, sage and the scapegoat for all mishaps. You might be forgiven for assuming this to be burden enough, but no! Its not widely known, except by the professional fraternity, that the caddie can serve two masters. Should he find himself in this dual role he'd better beware these complications; 'When one caddie is employed by more than one player, he is always deemed to be the caddie of the player whose ball is involved, and equipment carried by him is deemed to be that player's equipment, except when the caddie acts upon specific directions of another player, in which case he is deemed to be that other player's caddie'. Confused? W.S. has the laid-back answer—"Time must untangle this, not I 'tis too hard a knot for me to untie". (Twelfth Night)

The Caddie-Master addresses his flock

> *Who is here so base that would be a bondman ?*
> *If any, speak, for him have I offended.*

[Julius Caesar III ii 31]

It's a tough job

> *Who would fardels bear,*
> *To grunt and sweat under a weary life?*

[Hamlet III i 76]

A suitable candidate?

> *A duteous and knee-crooking knave*
> *That, doting on his own obsequious bondage,*
> *Wears out his time, much like his master's ass,*
> *For naught but .provender.*

[Othello I i 44]

Straws in the air seem to question his judgement.

> *Sits the wind in that Quarter?*

[Much Ado About Nothing II iii 108]

Another fine mess

> *Give me that mattock and the wrenching iron.*

[Romeo and Juliet V ii 23]

I said 200 yards, not metres!

> And if ought of this miscarry by my fault,
> Let my old life be sacrificed
> Unto the full rigour of the law.

[Romeo and Juliet V iii 265]

His error or mine?

> And where the offence is
> Let the great axe fall.

[Hamlet IV iv 220]

Magnanimous

> O this boy doth lend mettle to us all.

[Henry IV Pt I V iv 24]

A covetous caddie

> What would he do had he the motive
> And the cue for passion that I have.
> Yet I, a dull and muddy- mettled rascal peak and pine,
> Un pregnant of my cause.

[Hamlet II ii 594]

He's no chance

> A wretch whose gifts were poor
> To those of mine.

[Hamlet I v 52]

Caddie disagrees

> He does it with a better grace
> But I do it more natural

[Twelfth Night II iii 79]

Still resentful

> I am the drudge and toil in your delight.

[Romeo And Juliet II v 77]

Despite the weight of fourteen clubs

> O heavy burden.

[Hamlet III i 54]

Under sufferance

> For who would bear the whips and scorns of time,
> Th'oppressor's wrong,
> The proud man's contumely.

[Hamlet III i 87]

You owe me one!

> I have lost my teeth in your service.

[As You Like It I i 74]

Chapter 23: The Golf Widow

Mindful of the burgeoning number of lady golfers you might reasonably deduce that the golf widow was the relic of a bygone age. But no! They still exist, as magnanimous understanding, forgiving, long-suffering and patient as ever. Or are they?

Genuine or apocryphal, all these attributes were recognised by W,S.- And a few others as well.

Musings on togetherness
> *If I be left behind, a moth of peace and he go to the war,*
> *The rites for which I love him are bereft me,*
> *And I a heavy interim shall support by his dear absence*
>
> [Othello I iii 257]

I used to come first.
> *Dwell I but in the suburbs of your pleasure?*
>
> [Julius Caesar II i 285]

Have you forgotten?
> *That great vow that did incorporate and make us one.*
>
> [Julius Caesar II i 272]

Is this to be my lot?
> *Hast thou no care of me?*
> *Shall I abide in this dull world, which in thy absence*
> *Is no better than a sty?*
>
> [Antony and Cleopatra IV xv 100]

That's below the belt.
> *The lady doth protest too much methinks.*
>
> [Hamlet III ii 242]

Touching
> *The poor soul sat sighing,*
> *Sing all a green willow.*
>
> [Othello IV iii 41]

But don't fall for it
> *Her voice was ever soft, gentle and low,*
> *An excellent thing in woman.*
>
> [King Lear V iii 274]

Real colours begin to show
> *Do not presume too much upon my love,*
> *I may do that I shall be sorry for.*
>
> [Julius Caesar IV iii 63]

A loaded question

> For what offence have I this fortnight
> Been a banished woman ?

[Henry IV Pt.I. II iii 40]

Embryonic doubts

> Some heavy business hath my lord in hand,
> And I must know it or he love me not.

[Henry IV Pt.I. II iii 65]

The smiles have gone

> This look of thine will hurl my soul from heaven,.
> And thieves will snatch at it.

[Othello V ii 172]

Temperature's rising!

> O, when she is angry, she is keen and shrewd,
> And, though she is but little,
> She is fierce!

[A Midsummer Night's Dream III ii 323]

Try humouring

> Swear me Kate, like a lady as thou art,
> A good mouth-filling oath.

[Henry IV Pt.I. III i 253]

Fair point

> Let husbands know their wives have sense like them;
> They see and smell
> And have their palates both for sweet and sour
> As husbands have.

[Othello IV iii 91]

Hardening positions

> Fie upon this quiet life!
> I want work.

[Henry IV Pt.I II iv 116]

> You shall not stir out of your house to-day.

[Julius Caesar II ii 9]

A likely story

> I have more care to stay than will to go.

[Romeo And Juliet III v 23]

Getting desperate

> You go to do you know not what.

[Julius Caesar III ii 236]

You're normally so reasonable

Tis not in thee to grudge my pleasures.
To bandy hasty words.
To oppose the bolt against my coming in.
Thou better know'st the offices of nature,
The effects of courtesy, dues of gratitude.

[King Lear II iv 172]

Late home again

It is not meet that every nice offence,
Should bear this comment.

[Julius Caesar IV iii 7]

A lame excuse

My story being done
She gave me for my pains a world of sighs.
She swore in faith 'twas strange,
'Twas passing strange, 'twas pitiful,
'Twas wondrous pitiful.

[Othello I iii 158]

She'll not forget this one in a hurry

You are now sailed into the north of my lady's opinion;
Where you will hang like an icicle on a Dutchman's beard.

[Twelfth Night III ii 29]

It cannot be that serious

Should all despair that have revolted wives,
The tenth of mankind would hang themselves

[The Winter's Tale I ii 198]

Time to be assertive

Men at some time are masters of their fates.

[Julius Caesar I ii 139]

Is this the end then?

Leave her to heaven, and to the thorns
That in her bosom lodge to prick and sting her.

[Hamlet I v 86]

The crocodiles are at it again

Ere yet the salt of most unrighteous tears
Had left the flushing in her galled eyes.

[Hamlet I ii 154]

So what can you expect then?

Frailty, thy name is woman!

[Hamlet I ii 146]

For future reference

> And have not we affections, desires for sport,
> And frailty as men have?
> Then let them use us well; else let them know
> The ills we do, their ills instruct us so.

[Othello IV iii 98]

Once bitten

> Both here and hence pursue me lasting strife,
> If, once a widow, ever I be a wife.

[Hamlet III ii 217]

The perpetual enigma

> Age cannot wither her
> Nor custom stale her infinite variety.

[Antony and Cleopatra II ii 243]

Normal relationships resumed

> Either she hath bewitch'd me with her words,
> Or nature makes me suddenly relent.

[Henry VI Pt.I III iii 58]

> She never told her love, but let concealment
> Like a worm i'th'bud, feed on her damask cheek.
> She pined in thought.
> And with a green and yellow melancholy
> She sat like patience on a monument, smiling at grief.

[Twelfth Night II iv 108]

Chapter 24: The Ancient Royals

The brainchild of Alan Evans of the Royal Eastbourne, the 'Ancients' as they are affectionately called thereabouts corresponds rather grandly with the Veterans elsewhere. Uniquely, the Ancients play on two separate courses simultaneously, have a handicapping system which few understand but no-one dares to question (devised by Alan, alias'The Fuehrer, 'Evans) and play otherwise strictly to R.& A rules, if anyone can remember them! Play gives way to the presentation ritual, the winners receiving a ball hurled at them across the room from twenty paces. The occasion is also used to berate defaulters, usually for failing to appreciate that a handicap in this company has an infinitely variable life of its own and needs constant vigilance.

In common with veterans elsewhere the 'Ancients' are getting younger, stronger and more competent. No longer is thirty points a good enough score to guarantee winning that coveted ball. But, with an ever lengthening life span there are plenty of old-uns around, adding character, variety, experience and a diverting eccentricity to enliven the wider golf scene.

Was it from his latter-day association with the Veterans that W.S. was able to draw his more interesting characters?

From now on, it's for fun
> *Thou art not for the fashion of these times*
> *Where none will sweat but for promotion.*
>
> [As You Like It II iii 156]

A special Ancients format becomes necessary
> *Crabbed age and youth cannot live together.*
> *Youth is full of pleasure.*
> *Age is full of care.*
>
> [The Passionate Pilgrim]

It's a real puzzle
> *And can you by no drift of circumstance*
> *Get from him why he puts on this confusion.*
> *Grating so harshly all his days of quiet*
> *With turbulent and dangerous lunacy?*
>
> [Hamlet III i 1]

Possible answers

> *I am a very foolish, fond old man.*
> *Four score and upward, not an hour more nor less.*
> *And to deal plainly' I fear I am not in my perfect mind.*
>
> [King Lear IV vii 60]

A full eighteen holes could be just one too many

> *O sir, you are old.*
> *Nature in you stands on the very verge of her confine.*
>
> [King Lear II iv 148]

Until then, Cheers!

> *I have very poor and unhappy brains for drinking:*
> *I could well wish courtesy*
> *Would invent some other custom of entertainment.*
>
> [Othello II iii 30]

That's drink for you!

> *Second childishness and mere oblivion*
> *Sans teeth, sans eyes, sans taste*
> *Sans everything.*
>
> [As You Like It II vii 1]

He never was much cop

> *'Tis the infirmity of his age.*
> *Yet he hath ever but slenderly known himself.*
>
> [King Lear II i 292]

Age and over-golfing can be the cause

> *A plentiful lack of wit*
> *Together with most weak hams.*
>
> [Hamlet II ii 201]

He was great before arthritis and a third wife blew him off course

> *That unmatched figure of blown youth*
> *Blasted with ecstasy.*
>
> [Hamlet III i 159]

Accept your new limitations

> *Have you not a moist eye, a dry hand*
> *A yellow cheek, a white beard,*
> *A decreasing leg, an increasing belly?*
> *Is not your voice broken and your wind short*
> *Your chin double and your wit single*
> *And every part about you blasted with antiquity,*
> *And will you yet call yourself young?*
>
> [As You Like It II iii 156]

Self esteem's important

> *Perseverance keeps honour bright.*

[Troilus And Cressida III iii 15]

There must be an explanation

> *Why should our endeavour be so loved*
> *And our performance so loathed?*

[Troilus And Cressida V x 36]

Here it comes

> *Thou should'st not have been old*
> *Till thou had'st been wise.*

[King Lear I v 41]

Try to remember the basics

> *The unruly waywardness*
> *That infirm and choleric years bring with them..*

[King' Lear II i 298]

Aid is at hand

> *'Tis not enough to help the feeble up*
> *But to support him after.*

[Timon Of Athens I i 108]

What are friends for?

> *To ease them of their griefs*
> *Their fear of hostile strokes,*
> *Their aches, losses,*
> *That nature's fragile vessel doth sustain*
> *In life's uncertain voyage,*
> *I will some kindness do them.*

[Timon Of Athens V i 196]

Sad, but should have joined the 'Ancients' earlier.

> *My way of life is fallen into the sear, the yellow leaf.*
> *And that which should accompany old age,*
> *As honour, love, obedience,*
> *Troops of friends,*
> *I must not look to have.*

[Macbeth V iii 22]

And so,

> *You see me here you gods,*
> *A poor old man,*
> *As full of grief as age;*
> *Wretched in both.*

[King Lear II iv 271]

The retirement credo

> *If all the year were playing holidays*
> *To sport would be as tedious as to work*
> *But when they seldom come,*
> *They wished for come.*

[Henry IV Pt.I I ii 197]

Exclusive clique

> *This happy band of men, This little world.*

[Richard II II i 40]

The Alan Evan's legacy

> *This teeming womb of Royal kings,*
> *Feared by their breed*
> *And famous by their birth.*

[Richard II II i 51]

Chapter 25: Rub Of The Green

Theatre of the 'If only, but for, and may-be', the golf course has been blamed for more errors within the domain of its eighteen holes than you could aggregate from a whole world beyond it. What is more, the penalties accruing from these cruel misfortunes are on a gigantic scale. How many championships have hinged on the capricious last half turn of a ball, or the miniscule deviation as pace yields to bias or bias to pace. How often have bunkers gathered in the ball, perversely affected by wind, ricochet or bounce?

Acts of God, unlucky or inept, 'the rub' is the universal culprit. W.S. tells it as it is.

Cosmic influences

> *When we are sick in fortune,*
> *Oft' the surfeits of our own behaviour,*
> *We make guilty of our disasters,*
> *The sun, the moon and stars;*
> *As if we were villains of necessity;*
> *Fools by heavenly compulsion;*
> *Knaves, thieves and treachers,*
> *By spherical predominance.*

[King Lear I ii 126]

Wouldn't you know it

> *The world is full of rubs,*
> *And thus my fortune runs against the bias.*

[Richard II III iv 5]

Divine scapegoat

> *O God, thy arm was here!*

[Henry V IV viii 104]

Look to thyself

> *Our remedies oft' in ourselves do lie*
> *Which we ascribe to heaven.*

[All's Well That Ends Well I i 235]

Passing the buck

> *What folly I commit,*
> *I dedicate to you.*

[Troilus And Cressida. III ii 109]

Try again

> *Good reasons must, of force,*
> *Give place to better.*

[Julius Caesar IV iii 202]

It's all in the genes you see

> *If I chance to talk a little wild, forgive me;*
> *I had it from my father*

[Henry VIII I iv 26]

That's more like it

> *If sugar and sack be at fault,*
> *God help the wicked.*

[Henry IV Pt.I. 11 iv 524]

Learn from your mistakes

> *The injuries that wilful men procure'*
> *Must be their schoolmasters.*

[King Lear II iv 300]

And you could get lucky

> *Our indiscretion sometimes serves us well.*

[Hamlet V ii 8]

But don't bank on it

> *Virtue itself escapes not calumnious strokes.*

[Hamlet I iii 38]

Some get away with it

> *Use every man after his deserts*
> *And who shall 'scape whipping?*

[Hamlet II ii 5]

But never yours truly!

> *I am a man more sinned against*
> *Than sinning.*

[King Lear II ii 58]

Chapter 26: Foul-weather Golf

It is widely recognised that the most dangerous weather conditions for golf involve lightning storms. Should you be caught out in such conditions, the U.S. Golf Association advises that you seek shelter in, a cave, a depression in the ground, a deep valley or canyon, or the foot of a steep or overhanging cliff. As these geological features are strangers to the typical golfing landscape, it is the common belief that the relevant U.S.P.G.A. committee had spent the previous night 'burning' through a deeply impressionable performance of King Lear. Let's see how W.S.influenced them.

Prospects of play not good
> *I never saw the heavens so dim by day.*
>
> [The Winters Tale III iii 55]

It's only a friendly four ball!
> *The heavens with that we have in hand are angry.*
>
> [The Winters Tale III iii 5]

Play abandoned
> *Is there no play to ease the anguish*
> *Of a torturing hour?*
>
> [Midsummer Night's Dream V i 3]

Indefinitely
> *For the rain it raineth every day.*
>
> [Twelfth Night V i 401]

Boring alternatives
> *Sweet recreation barr'd, what doth ensue*
> *But moody and dull melancholy.*
>
> [Comedy of Errors V i 7]

Intermittent breaks
> *So fair and foul a day I have not seen.*
>
> [Macbeth I ii 58]

Dark forebodings
> *Coal-black clouds*
> *That shadow heaven's light.*
> *Do summon us to part.*
>
> [Venus and Adonis 532]

Two to one we'll get wet

> *The storm is up and all is on the hazard.*

> [Julius Caesar V iv 6]

Poor visibility

> *Fair is foul and foul is fair,*
> *Hover through the fog and filthy air.*

> [Macbeth I i 1]

This should clear the fog

> *Blow winds and crack your cheeks*
> *Rage, blow you cataracts and hurricanoes spout.*

> [King Lear III ii 1]

Hold on to your hats

> *The splitting wind makes flexible*
> *The knees of knotted oaks.*

> [Troilus and Cressida I iii 49]

And your guts

> *Rumble thy bellyful! Spit; fire; spout, rain.*

> [King Lear III ii 14]

I was playing badly anyway

> *I tax not you, you elements, with unkindness;*
> *You owe me no subscription.*
> *Then let fall your horrible pleasure.*
> *Here I stand, your slave. O ho! 'tis foul.*

> [King Lear III ii 14]

Steady as a rock

> *Are you not mov'd, when all the sway of earth*
> *Shakes like a thing unfirm?*

> [Julius Caesar I iii 3]

And thick skinned to boot

> *Was this a face*
> *To be oppos'd against the warring winds ?*
> *To stand against the deep dread-bolted thunder?*

> [King Lear IV vii 32]

Facing such awesome opponents

> *Either there is civil strife in heaven,*
> *Or else the world, too saucy with the gods,*
> *Incenses them to send destruction.*

> [Julius Caesar I iii 11]

What other challenges could you want?

> *Here shall he see*
> *No enemy*
> *But winter and rough weather.*

[As You Like It II v 39]

Trapped out in the far reaches of the course

> *How, in this our pinching cave shall we discourse ,*
> *The freezing hours away.*

[Cymbeline III iii 37]

It can't last forever! - Can it?

> *Come what come may,.*
> *Time and the hour runs through the roughest day.*

[Macbeth I iii 147]

> *Distracted clouds give way*
> *So stand thou forth, the time is fair again.*

All's Well That Ends Well V iii 47]

Let's talk 'temperatures'

> *The air bites shrewdly; it is very cold.*

[Hamlet I iv 1]

Agreed!

> *'Tis bitter cold, and I am sick at heart.*

[Hamlet I i 8]

I concur!

> *It is a nipping and an eager air.*

[Hamlet I iv 2]

I've just said that!

> *It is a nipping and an eager air.*

[Hamlet I iv 2]

How about some mixed metaphors?

> *Let the sky rain potatoes;*
> *Let it thunder to the tune of Greensleeves*
> *Hail kissing comfits and snow eryngoes.*
> *Let there come a tempest of provocation*
> *I'll shelter me here.*

[Merry Wives of Windsor V v 22]

And something completely different

> *Love comforteth like sunshine after rain,*
> *But lust's effect is tempest after sun;*
> *Love's gentle Spring doth always fresh remain;*
> *Lust's Winter comes ere Summer's half be done.*

[Venus and Adonis 799]

But seriously

> *How is it that the clouds,*
> *Still hang on you?*

[Hamlet I ii 73]

So that's all right then.

> *I am but mad north-north- west;*
> *When the wind is southerly I know a hawk from a handsaw.*

[Hamlet II ii 374]

It's been interesting; let's do it again sometime.

> *When shall we three meet again?*
> *In thunder, lightning, or in rain?*

[Macbeth I i 1]

Chapter 27: The Final Farewell

The time comes when alternatives run out and hanging up your boots is the ultimate imperative. Age and infirmity have taken their toll, leaving the golfer with a rag-bag of nostalgic memories and unfulfilled dreams. It's the same now as it ever was, despite the sophistry of the joker who hypothesised, 'Nostalgia isn't what it used to be'. Let us see if W.S. agrees

Why did I ever listen to that golfing guru?

>   *The red plague rid you*
>   *For learning me your language!*

                                          [The Tempest I ii 363]

Quid pro quo

>   *As you from crimes would pardoned be,*
>   *Let your indulgence set me free.*

                                          [The Tempest. Epilogue]

The vital ingredient

>   *So long as men can breathe or eyes can see,*
>   *So long lives this, and this gives life to thee.*

                                          [Sonnet 18]

Some regrets,

>   *Farewell the tranquil mind! Farewell content!*
>   *Farewell pride pomp and circumstance of glorious war!*

                                          [Othello III iii 352]

Sic transit gloria mundi

>   *The painful warrior famoused for fight,*
>   *After a thousand victories once foil'd,*
>   *Is from the book of honour razed quite,*
>   *And all the rest forgot for which he toil'd.*

                                          [Sonnet 25]

Love's labours lost

>   *When to the sessions of sweet silent thought*
>   *I summon up remembrance of things past,*
>   *I sigh the lack of many a thing I sought,*
>   *And with old woes new wail my dear time's waste.*

                                          [Sonnet 30]

Time for clearing out the clutter
> *Yea, from the table of my memory*
> *I'll wipe away all trivial fond records,*
> *All saws of books, all forms, all pressures past,*
> *That youth and observation copied there.*

[Hamlet I v 98]

The hurt is over
> *Fear no more the heat o'th' sun,*
> *Nor the furious winter's rages;*
> *Thou thy worldly task hast done,*
> *Home art gone and ta'en thy wages,*
> *Golden lads and girls all must,*
> *As chimney-sweepers, come to dust.*

[Cymbeline IV ii 259]

Welcome oblivion
> *Weary and old with service, to the mercy*
> *Of a rude stream, that must for ever hide me.*

[Henry VIII III ii 363]

Do me justice
> *Report me and my cause aright to the unsatisfied.*

[Hamlet V iii 353]

O.K. If you insist, but the truth might hurt.
> *A poor player, that struts and frets his hour upon the stage,*
> *And then is heard no more.*

[Macbeth V v 23]

There's no answer to that
> *The rest is silence!*

[Hamlet V iii 372]

Chapter 28: Consolation

Its only a game or,. Its more than a game, its a way of life- just two of the well-worn clichés from the world of sport, both outflanked from the soccer world by, "Its not a matter of life and death; its more important than that". It is no accident that these aphorisms are invariably applied to team games where the joys and sorrows of success and failure are shared by others. Golf provides no such succour or mutual comfort. The golfer, perforce, suffers alone.
So what can W.S. offer to lift the gloom?

Inconsolable

> *He receives comfort like cold porridge.*

[The Tempest II i 10]

Voice of experience

> *Everyone can master grief*
> *But he that has it.*

[Much Ado About Nothing III ii 28]

Recovery can be a long haul

> *Take comfort of all my library,*
> *And so beguile thy sorrow.*

[Titus Andronicus IV i 34]

The sticking plaster solution

> *Patch grief with proverbs.*

[Much Ado About Nothing V i 17]

Stoicism isn't what it used to be

> *There was never yet philosopher*
> *That could endure toothache patiently.*

[Much Ado About Nothing V i 35]

So its best you keep losing for a while

> *They say best men.*
> *Are moulded out of faults;*
> *Better for being a little bad.*

[Measure For Measure V i 440]

Let it all hang out

> *0 now you weep,*
> *And I perceive you feel the dint of pity.*
> *These are gracious drops.*

[Julius Caesar III ii 188]

Go easy on him

> *Breathe his faults so quaintly*
> *That they seem the taints of liberty;*
> *The flash and outbreak of a fiery mind.*

[Hamlet II i 31]

Show compassion

> *Glancing an eye of pity on his losses,*
> *That have of late so huddled on his back.*

[Merchant Of Venice IV i 27]

A trouble shared

> *A friend should bear his friend's infirmities.*

[Julius Caesar IV iii 85]

Try damning the fault with faint praise

> *Though it lacked form a little.*
> *Was not like madness.*

[Hamlet III i 163]

A perverted response

> *All strange and terrible events are welcome,*
> *But comforts we despise.*

[Antony and Cleopatra IV xv 3]

So try reproach

> *I must be cruel only to be kind.*

Hamlet III iv 178]

Avoid humour

> *Mirth cannot move a soul in agony.*

[Love's Labour's Lost V ii 937]

Lower your sights a little

> *The apprehension of the good*
> *Gives but the greater feeling to the worse.*

[Richard II I iii 294]

This might make you feel better

> *Oft expectation fails, and most oft there*
> *Where most it promises; and oft it hits*
> *Where hope is coldest, and despair most fits.*

[All's Well That Ends Well II i 141]

Chapter 29: Winning Is All

For the less gifted golfer winning can be a rare event. He accepts as normal therefore that he forks out on a regular basis, the one pound on the match, the twenty pence birdies and sundry other bits and pieces. These recurrent attacks on the wallet have long been budgeted for in the weekly housekeeping. By contrast, the un-looked for bonus of actually winning is to flood his life with sunshine. But, wouldn't you know it! the euphoria is dashed by the crestfallen countenance of an opponent for whom winning is paramount. His misery is such that you would gladly find some pretext to reverse the result and restore his grim features to that smug, self-satisfied expression that winning has accustomed them to. He, of course suffers no such pangs of remorse. A stranger to scruples, he employs all the deft cunning he can muster, while you, poor fool would rather lose the hole by intent than have him 'pick up his bat' and head for home in high dudgeon.

W.S. was likewise vulnerable, but, in general, pulled out all the stops to win.

The winners' charter

> *How much better it is to weep at joy than to joy at weeping*
>> [Much Ado About Nothing I i 24]

An easy prey

> *Here comes the trout that must be caught with ticklin.g*
>> [Twelfth Night II v 20]

I've detected his Achilles heel

> *If I can catch him once upon the hip,*
> *I will feed fat the ancient grudge I bear him.*
>> [Merchant of Venice I iii 41]

Savouring revenge

> *I do begin to have bloody thoughts.*
>> [The Tempest IV i 220]

Winning dubiously

> *Thou hast it now; and I fear*
> *Thou play'dst most foully for't.*
>> [Macbeth III i 1]

Cheats never prosper

> *The whirligig of time brings in his revenges.*
>> [Twelfth Night V i 363]

91

Power corrupts

> *I grow; I prosper.*
> *Now, gods stand up for bastards.*

[King Lear I ii 21]

It's not all down to skill

> *Luck in very spite of cunning,*
> *Bade him win all.*

[Troilus and Cressida V v 42]

Winning is no big deal !

> *Men prize the thing ungained more than it is.*

[Troilus and Cressida I ii 31]

Machiavellian tendencies

> *Then with the losers let it sympathise,*
> *For nothing can seem foul to those that win.*

[Henry IV Pt.I V i 9]

No quarter given

> *Doubly redoubled strokes upon the foe.*
> *Except they meant to bathe in reeking wounds;*
> *Or memorize another Golgotha,*
> *I cannot tell.*

[Macbeth I ii 38]

The Olympic spirit

> *Things won are done; joy's soul lies in the doing.*

[Troilus And Cressida I ii 310]

Playing by the rules always triumphs

> *Corruption wins not more than honesty.*

[Henry VIII III ii 441]

Try witchcraft

> *Look, with a spot I damn him.*

[Julius Caesar IV I 6]

The preliminary handshake

> *Though I do hate him as I do hell pains,*
> *Yet for the necessity of present life,*
> *I must show out a flag of love.*

[Othello I ii 1]

The declined handshake

> *I do desire we may be better strangers.*

[As You Like It III ii 283]

A doughty opponent

> *Jealous in honour*
> *Sudden and quick in quarrel.*

[As You Like It II vii 151]

I have a point to prove

> *I am one,*
> *Whom the vile blows and buffets of the world*
> *Have so incensed, that I am reckless what I do*
> *To spite the world.*

[Macbeth III i 106]

But have you no compassion?

> *The eagle suffers little birds to sing.*

[Titus Andronicus IV iv 85]

Would you encourage wickedness?

> *Nothing emboldens sin*
> *So much as mercy .*

[Timon of Athens III v 4]

You make me angry

> *Come not within the measure of my wrath.*

[Two Gentleman of Verona V iv128]

And a fearless trophy hunter

> *Bell book and candle shall not drive me back*
> *When gold and silver*
> *Becks me to come on.*

[King John III I 12]

So, no holds barred

> *Let us to it pell-mell;*
> *If not to heaven,*
> *Then hand in hand to hell.*

[Richard III V iii 312]

Putting off the coup de grace

> *But I am pigeon-liver'd and lack gall,*
> *Or ere this,*
> *I should 'a fatted all the region kites*
> *With this slave's offal.*   .

[Hamlet II ii 57]

He'll still need watching

> *Such men as he be never at heart's ease*
> *Whiles they behold a greater than themselves,*
> *And therefore are they very dangerous.*

[Julius Caesar I ii 207]

But in the end we're all just a bunch of losers

> *He that filches from me my good name*
> *Robs me of that which not enriches him*
> *And makes me poor indeed.*

[Othello III iii 163]

Chapter 30 Early Morning Golf

At no other time of day does the golf course look so inviting. The tranquil solitude in the early morning sunshine, augmenting the manicured outlines of tees and greens, edged with overnight dew, all beckon you to a faultless round.

At such times it would be incongruous to greet your playing partner with the customary 'morning Fred' The ambience invites a more poetic salutation in harmony with the idyllic setting and aptly portraying the pervading enchantment. Any ideas? W.S. has, because, "Many a morning hath he there been seen, with tears augmenting the fresh morning dew"- (Romeo and Juliet)

Good morrow, masters; put your torches out;
The wolves have prey'd; and look, the gentle day,
Before the wheels of Phoebus, round about
Dapples the drowsy east with spots of gray.

[Much Ado About Nothing V iii 24]

Night's candles are burnt out, and jocund day
Stands tiptoe on the misty mountain tops.

[Romeo And Juliet III v 9]

But look, the morn, in russet mantle clad,
Walks o'er the dew of yon high eastern hill.

[Hamlet I i 166]

The glowworm shows the matin to be near,
And gins to pale his ineffectual fire.

[Hamlet I v 89]

Hark, hark! the lark at heaven's gate sings,
And Phoebus 'gins arise.

[Cymbeline II iii 22]

The grey-ey'd morn smiles on the frowning night,
Check' ring the eastern clouds with streaks of light;
And fleckel'd darkness like a drunkard reels
From forth day's path and Titan's fiery wheels.
Now, ere the sun advance his burning eye
The day to cheer and night's dank dew to dry

[Romeo And Juliet II iii 1]

The air nimbly and sweetly recommends itself
Unto our gentle senses.

[Macbeth I vi 2]

The cock, that is the trumpet to the morn,
Doth with his lofty and shrill-sounding throat
Awake the god of day.

[Hamlet I i 148]

This battle fares like to the morning's war,
When dying clouds contend with growing light.

[Henry VI Pt III II v 1]

How bloodily the sun begins to peer
Above yon busky hill! The day looks pale
At his distemp'rature..

[Henry IV Pt.I V i 1]

A glooming peace this morning with it brings;
The sun for sorrow will not show his head.
Go hence, to have more talk of these sad things;
Some shall be pardon'd and some punished.

[Romeo and Juliet V iii 303]

Chapter 31: A Game Of Love

Magnanimity is a difficult precept to follow in the normal course of everyday life. It's no easier on the golf course. By nature, golf is a contest, a running battle ,and you arm yourself appropriately with the weapons to prove it. You win some, and you lose some, and some losses hurt more than others. In particular, you could have waited a long time to avenge a previous indignity.

W.S. had little time for games played for love; hence the more likely challenge - Have at you!

Opening shots

> *If you prick us do we not bleed?*
> *And if you wrong us shall we not revenge?*
>
> [The Merchant Of Venice III i 53]

> *The villainy you teach me I will execute;*
> *And it shall go hard but I will better*
> *The instruction.*
>
> [The Merchant Of Venice III I 62]

So tread softly

> *Thou hast not half the power to do me harm*
> *As I have to be hurt.*
>
> [Othello V i 164]

Or you could regret it

> *Press not a falling man too far*
>
> [Henry VIII 11ii 416]

Lest your deeds return to haunt you

> *Heat not a furnace for your foe so hot*
> *That it do singe yourself.*
>
> [Henry VIII I i 140]

That's enough temporizing`

> *Come not between the dragon and his wrath.*
>
> [King Lear I i 121]

The mind boggles. What can it be?

> *Though I am, not splenetive and rash,*
> *Yet have I in me something dangerous,*
> *Which let thy wiseness fear.*
>
> [Hamlet V i 255]

Is that all?

> *You spit on me on Wednesday last.*
> *You spurn'd me such a day;*
> *Another time you called me dog.*

[The Merchant Of Venice I iii 124]

The sovereign remedy

> *Let's make us medicine of our great revenge*
> *To cure this deadly grief.*

[Macbeth IV iii 21]

Breaking the code

> *To know our enemies' minds we'd rip their hearts.*

[King Lear IV vi 262]

To be honest, we're well matched

> *A knave, beggar, coward, pander,*
> *And the son and heir of a mongrel bitch;*
> *One whom I will beat into clamorous whining.*

[King Lear II ii 18]

Despite setbacks

> *How all occasions do inform against me.*
> *And spur my dull revenge.*

[Hamlet IV iv 32]

To give me a slight advantage

> *Make thick my blood*
> *Stop up the access and passage to remorse,*
> *That no compunctious visitings of nature*
> *Shake my fell purpose.*

[Macbeth I v 40]

And that's only a nine iron

> *Disdaining fortune with his brandished steel*
> *Which smoked with bloody execution.*

[Macbeth I ii 1]

Well, an eight perhaps

> *I took by the throat the uncircumcised dog.*
> *And smote him - thus.*

[Othello V ii 358]

Not quite 'sudden' death

> *May his pernicious soul rot,*
> *Half a grain a day.*

[Othello V ii 158]

Envy

> O! beware of jealousy;
> It is the green-eyed monster which doth mock
> The meat it feeds on.

[Othello III iii 165]

We all have feelings

> The smallest worm will turn being trodden on.

[Henry VI Pt 11 II ii 22]

A disarming riposte

> I have not from your eyes that gentleness
> And show of love
> That I was wont to have.

[Julius Caesar I ii 3]

You're a real puzzle

> I do fear thy nature; It is too full o'th' milk
> Of human kindness;
> Wouldst not play false,
> And yet wouldst wrongly win.

[Macbeth I v 13]

A friendly warning

> Take heed of yonder dog!
> Look when he fawns, he bites; and when he bites,
> His venom tooth will rankle to the death;
> Have not to do with him, beware of him;
> Sin, death, and hell, have set their mark on him

[Richard III I iii 335]

So, keep your eye on the ball!

> Like to the Pontic sea,
> Whose icy current and compulsive course
> Ne'er feels retiring ebb, but keeps due on
> To the Propontic and the Hellespont;
> Even so my bloody thoughts, with violent pace,
> Shall ne'er look back, ne'er ebb to humble love,
> Till that a capable and wide revenge
> Swallow them up.

[Othello III iii 456]

A charitable afterthought

> Love thyself last,
> Cherish those hearts that hate thee.

[Henry V111 III ii 44]

The abiding golf enigma

My only love sprung from my only hate.

[Romeo and Juliet I v 136]

Chapter 32: Self – Chastisement

To censure oneself for mistakes made on the golf course is common practice. It normally takes the form of a metaphorical slap on the wrist, accompanied by a variety of homespun, sotto voce mutterings, and all emanating from a minor lapse of concentration. Let it be admitted however that there are golfers who go over the top. For them the mild self-reproach is alien, and any mistake is so heinous as to promote a tirade of self-abuse that puts them quite beyond consolation. Resort to suicide is rare, though if threats translated into deeds, many would come close to premature demise. 'Words, words' as W.S. has it.

Blow me about in winds! roast me in sulphur!
Wash me in steep-down gulfs of liquid fire!

[Othello V ii 282]

Beat at this gate that let thy folly in
And thy dear judgement out.

[King Lear I iv 160]

I have lost my reputation!
I have lost the immortal part of myself,
And what remains is bestial.

[Othello II iii 264]

I am bound upon a wheel of fire
That mine own tears do scald like molten lead.

[King Lear IV vii 46]

O, my offence is rank, it smells to heaven.

[Hamlet III iii 36]

Howl, howl, howl, howl! O you are men of stones!
Had I your tongues and eyes, I'd use them so
That heaven's vault should crack.

[King Lear V iii 257]

I am myself indifferent honest, but yet
I could accuse me of such things
That it were better my mother had not borne me.

[Hamlet III i 124]

Such a want-wit sadness makes of me
That I have much ado to know myself.

[The Merchant Of Venice I i 6]

Those wounds heal ill
That men do give themselves.

[Troilus And Cressida III iii 229]

Chapter 33: Epitaphs To Golfers

It is sad to relate that bidding farewell to a lifetime of golf is all too often the immediate precursor to shuffling off this mortal coil altogether. In fact, there are those who claim there's a cause and effect relationship. Reminiscences crowd in on the aftermath of these sad events and silent thoughts distil a lifetime into a few golden moments. Such is the meat of many an epitaph, while there are some who, wittingly or not, have written their own

Epigrammatic versions are the tour de force of W.S.

An honest-to-goodness eighteen handicapper

Speak of me as I am;
Nothing extenuate,
Nor set down aught in malice.
Then must you speak
Of one who loved not wisely but too well.

[Othello V ii 344]

I was on the Greens Committee in 1924.

I have done the state some service, and they know't
No more of that.

[Othello V ii 342]

Scatter my ashes on the course

Heaven take my soul,
And England keep my bones!

[King John IV iii 10]

The model golfer

His life was gentle;
And the elements,
So mixed in him,
That nature might stand up
And say to all the world,
'This was a man!'

[Julius Caesar V v 73]

A 'fruity' disposition

Men must endure their going hence,
Even as their coming hither:
Ripeness is all.

[King Lear V ii 9]

A world class golfer

> *When that this body did contain a spirit,*
> *A kingdom for it was far too small a bound*
> *But now two paces of the vilest earth*
> *Is room enough. This earth that bears thee dead*
> *Bears not alive so stout a gentleman.*

[Henry IV Pt.1 V iv 89]

A seven days a week golfer

> *I wasted time, and now doth time waste me*

[Richard II V v 49]

He was never a well man

> *After life's fitful fever he sleeps well;*
> *Nothing can touch him further.*

[Macbeth III ii 23]

Forget the score cards

> *Ignominy sleep with thee in the grave,*
> *But not rememb'red in thy epitaph!*

[HenryIV Pt.I V iv 100]

They don't matter any more

> *So may he rest;*
> *His faults lie gently on him!*

[HenryVIII IV ii 31]

A badly timed demise!

> *'A took my father grossly, full of bread,*
> *With all his crimes broad blown,*
> *And how his audit stands*
> *Who knows save heaven.*

[Hamlet III iii 80]

Where are your gibes now?

> *This counsellor is now most still,*
> *Most secret, and most grave,*
> *Who was in life a foolish prating knave.*

[Hamlet III iv 213]

That it should come to this!

> *His promises were, as he then was, mighty;*
> *But his performance, as he is now, nothing.*

[Henry VIII IV ii 57]

I've known worse golfers
> *Farewell!*
> *I could have better spar'd a better man.*
>
> [Henry IV PT.I V iv 102]

A spectacular exit
> *Nothing in his life*
> *Became him like the leaving of it.*
>
> [Macbeth I iv 7]

A compulsive golfer
> *Speak of one that loved*
> *Not wisely, but too well.*
>
> [Othello V ii 347]

On his deathbed, still obsessed with golf courses
> *His nose was as sharp as a pen*
> *And a'babbled of green fields.*
>
> [Henry V II iii 9]

The golfing gourmand
> *The grave doth gape for thee*
> *Thrice wider than for other men*
>
> [Henry IVPt II V v 54]

Too sensitive for constant failure
> *A wretched soul,*
> *Bruised with adversity*
>
> [Comedy of Errors II i 34]

Over indulgent celebration was his undoing
> *Violent delights*
> *Have violent ends.*
>
> [Romeo and Juliet II v 9]

Life's a bitch!
> *The evil that men do lives after them;*
> *The good is oft'Interred in heir bones*
>
> [Julius Caesar III ii 75]

Not the most popular Club member
> *Here lie I*
> *Who alive all living men did hate*
> *Pass by, and curse thy fill; but pass*
> *And stay not here thy gait*
>
> [Timon of Athens V iv 90]

On the whole a good hombre
> *'A was a man, take him for all in all*
> *I shall not see his-like again.*

[Hamlet I ii 187]

Beyond contradiction
> *We have seen better days.*

[As You Like It II vii 119]

They cannot touch you now
> *You were better have a bad epitaph*
> *Than an ill report while you live.*

[Hamlet II ii 553]

Golf talent speaks for itself
> *A good play needs no epilogue.*

[As You Like It III ii 182]

Chapter 34: Honour

In truth, a fair number of golfers must be more accustomed to the words 'your honour' as a mode of address in the law court than as an invitation to tee off on the golf course. Tail end Charlie is more their station in life, and to have earned promotion by actually winning a hole is a culture shock of some magnitude. Any road up, as golfers not a million miles from Stratford might say, the word has other associations. W.S. concurs.

Winning's not everything

> *Good name in man and woman dear my lord,*
> *Is the immediate jewel of their souls.*

[Othello III iii 159]

Honour - the down side

> *Honour pricks me on.*
> *Yea, but how if honour pricks me off when I come on?*
> *What is honour? A word.*
> *Who hath it? He that died o'Wednesday.*
> *Doth he feel it? No. Doth he hear it? No*
> *'Tis insensible, then? Yea, to the dead.*
> *But will it not live with the living? No .Why?*
> *Detraction will not suffer it.*
> *Therefore I'll none of it.*
> *Honour is a mere scutcheon.*
> *And so ends my catechism.*

[Henry 1V Pt.I V i 130]

A cavalier attitude

> *Set honour in one eye and death i'th'other*
> *And I will look on both indifferently.*

[Julius Caesar I ii 86]

Other priorities

> *He after honour hunts, I after love.*

[Two Gentlemen of Verona I i 63]

Unimaginable event

> *It is an honour that I dream not of.*

[Romeo and Juliet I iii 67]

In pursuit of a forbidden fruit

> *If it be a sin to covet honour*
> *I am the most offending soul alive.*

[Henry V IV iii 28]

Play for keeps

See that you come
Not that you woo honour, but to wed it.

[All's Well That Ends Well II i 14]

However dishonourably won

An honour snatched with boist'rous. hand.

[Henry IV Pt.II IV v 192]

Over-reaction

Take honour from me, and my life is done.

[Richard II I i 177]

Honour dearly bought

I like not such grinning honour
As Sir Walter hath.

[Henry IV Pt.I V iii 61]

Fickle honour

Is't possible? No sooner got but lost?

[Troilus and Cressida IV ii 73]

It never gets any easier

By heaven, methinks it were an easy leap
To pluck bright honour from the pale-fac'd moon;
Or dive into the bottom of the deep,
Where fathom-line could never touch the ground,
And pluck up drowned honour by the locks;
So he that doth redeem her thence might wear
Without corrival all her dignities.

[Henry IV Pt.I I iii 200]

Chapter 35: Dejection

For companionship, for exercise, for fun- just a few reasons put forward by golfers to justify knocking the living daylights out of the innocent object of their derision, scorn and hate; then proceeding in varying degrees of haste to catch up to do it all over again. Putting aside these sadistic exercises, the 'fun' bit is not all that immediately obvious either. One errant shot, one mishit, and heaven forfend, one airshot is enough to plunge any self-respecting golfer into a pit of despair. Unadulterated pleasure - forget it! along with W.S.

> *I have of late-but wherefore I know not-lost all my mirth,*
> *Forgone all custom of exercises;*
> *And indeed it goes so heavily with my disposition*
> *That this goodly frame, the earth, seems to me*
> *A sterile promontory.*
>
> [Hamlet II ii 29]
>
> *Why, what's the matter*
> *That you have such a February face,*
> *So full of frost, of storm ,and cloudiness?*
>
> [Much Ado About Nothing V iv 39]
>
> *My mind is troubled like a fountain stirred;*
> *And I myself see not the bottom of it.*
>
> [Troilus and Cressida III iii 30]
>
> *How is it that the clouds still hang on you?*
>
> [Hamlet I ii 66]
>
> *In sooth, I know not why I am so sad.*
> *It wearies me; you say it wearies you;*
> *But how I caught it, found it, or came by it,*
> *What stuff 'tis made of, where it is born*
> *I am to learn.*
>
> [The Merchant Of Venice I i 1]
>
> *Would I were in an alehouse in London!*
> *I would give all my fame for a pot of ale.*
>
> [Henry V III ii 11]
>
> *I hold the world but as the world,*
> *A stage, where every man must play a part*
> *And mine a sad one.*
>
> [The Merchant of Venice I i 77]

If it were now to die'twere now to be most happy.

[Othello II i 187]

Adieu! I have too griev'd a heart
To take a tedious leave;
Thus losers part.

[Henry VI Pt II I iv 80]

How weary, stale, flat and unprofitable
Seem to me all the uses of this world.

[Hamlet I ii 142]

Let me have a dram of poison, such soon-speeding gear
As will disperse itself through all the veins
That the life-weary taker may fall dead,
And that the trunk may be discharged of breath.

[Romeo And Juliet V iii 116]

Come, bitter conduct, come, unsavoury guide,
Thou desperate pilot, now at once run on
The dashing rocks thy sea-sick weary bark.

[Romeo And Juliet V i 59]

Farewell the tranquil mind; farewell content!

[Othello III iii 352]

Chapter 36: Keeping A Cool Head

Some golfers have everything going for them; native talent, physique, raw good health, opportunity, and all that a silver spoon can feed to them from birth. When the Almighty was dishing out these goodies, alas the rest of us were firmly glued to the rear-most pews. Despite such inauspicious starters however, some manage to grind their way to the top. So what's the secret? Hard graft, practice, perseverance, dedication? It may well be all of these but W.S. suggests another ingredient- A cool head, in adversity.

> O, let me not be mad, not mad, sweet heaven;
> Keep me in temper; I would not be mad !
>
> [King Lear I v 43]
>
> Shall I be frighted when a madman stares?
>
> [Julius Caesar I v ii 40]
>
> Down, down thou climbing sorrow,
> Thy element's below.
>
> [King Lear II iv 56]
>
> Not soon provok'd, nor being provok'd, soon calmed.
>
> [Troilus and Cressida IV v 98]
>
> Give thy thoughts no tongue,
> Nor any unproportioned thought his act.
>
> [Hamlet I iii 59]
>
> The brain may devise laws for the blood,
> But a hot temper leaps o'er a cold decree.
>
> [The Merchant Of Venice I ii 12]
>
> Give me that man that is not passion's slave,
> And I will wear him in my heart's core.
>
> [Hamlet III ii 68]
>
> Whether 'tis nobler in the mind to suffer
> The slings and arrows of outrageous fortune,
> Or to take arms against a sea of troubles,
> And by opposing end them.
>
> [Hamlet III i 57]
>
> Meantime forbear, and let mischance
> Be slave to patience.
>
> [Romeo And Juliet V iii 219]

Good bawcock, bate thy rage
Use lenity, sweet chuck.

[Henry V III ii 24]

Yoked with a lamb, that carries anger
As the flint bears fire;
Who, much enforced, shows a hasty spark,
And straight is cold again.

[Julius Caesar IV iii 109]

Upon the heat and flame of thy distemper
Sprinkle cool patience.

[Hamlet III iv 123]

Chapter 37: Ambition

Cracking a hundred, eighteen handicap, single figures, scratch. Such are the progressive aspirations of youth. Though attained by some, for most golfers the vision fades, giving way to a more mature acceptance of mediocrity as the norm. New yardsticks provide attainable targets and the average golfer can settle down to a friendly Sunday four ball with the satisfying prospect of standing the first round out of his winnings. W.S. has found himself in just such a situation from time to time.

Optimism rewarded

> To day he puts forth
> The tender leaves of hopes, tomorrow blossoms,
> And bears his blushing honours thick upon him
>
> [Henry VIII III ii 352]

Smart-Ass

> But 'tis common proof
> That lowliness is young ambition's ladder
> Whereto the climber upward turns his face;
> But when he once attains the upmost round,
> He then unto the ladder turns his back,
> Looks in the clouds, scorning the base degrees
> By which he did ascend.
>
> [Julius Caesar II i 21]

Nemesis

> And when he thinks his greatness is a-ripening
> A killing frost nips his root,
> And then he falls.
>
> [Henry VIII III ii 352]

Overreaching folly

> I have no spur
> To prick the sides of my intent, but only
> Vaulting ambition, which o'er-leaps itself,
> And falls on th'other (side)
>
> [Macbeth I vii 24]

As night follows day

> Pride went before,
> Ambition followed him.
>
> [Henry VI Pt II I i 174]

Unquenchable thirst

> *I have immortal longings in me.*
>
> [Antony and Cleopatra V ii 282]

Unattainable targets

> *For who digs hills because they do aspire,*
> *Throws down one mountain*
> *To cast up a higher.*
>
> [Pericles I iv 5]

Work to a game plan

> *Ill-weaved ambition how much art thou shrunk.*
>
> [Henry IV Pt.I. V iv 87]

It's a long haul

> *Is it not strange*
> *That desire should so many years outlive performance.*
>
> [Henry IV Pt.II. II iv 250]

Fatal error

> *The hind that would be mated by the lion*
> *Must die for love.*
>
> [All's Well That Ends Well I i 84]

Timing a vital factor

> *There is a tide in the affairs of men*
> *Which, taken at the flood, leads on to fortune;*
> *Omitted, all the voyage of their life*
> *Is bound in shallows and in miseries.*
> *On such a full sea are we now afloat,*
> *And we must take the current when it serves,*
> *Or lose our ventures.*
>
> [Julius Caesar IV iii 216]

Taking stock

> *Lord, we know what we are, but know not what we may be.*
>
> [Hamlet IV v 41]

Forget single figures

> *Fling away ambition:*
> *By that sin fell the angels.*
> *How can man then,*
> *The image of his Maker, hope to win by it?*
>
> [Henry VIII III ii 439]

It's no big deal

> *Things won are done; joy's soul lies in the doing.*
>
> [Troilus and Cressida I ii 310]

114

A success too far

> *I have ventur'd,*
> *Like little wanton boys that swim on bladders*
> *This many summers in a sea of glory;*
> *But far beyond my depth.*
> *My high-blown pride*
> *At length broke under me,*
> *And now has left me,*
> *Weary and old to the mercy,*
> *Of a rude stream that must for ever hide me*

[Henry VIII III ii 358]

The surprising under achiever

> *Th'expectancy and rose of the fair state,*
> *The glass of fashion and the mould of form,*
> *Th'observed of all observers*
> *Quite, quite down!*

[Hamlet III i 152]

What to aim for? It's a lottery

> *If you can look into the seeds of time*
> *And say which grain will grow*
> *And which will not.*
> *Speak then to me who neither beg nor fear*
> *Your favours nor your hate.*

[Macbeth I iii 58]

Not for wimps!

> *Ambition should be made of sterner stuff.*

[Julius Caesar III ii 92]

Success can cause insomnia

> *Uneasy lies the head that wears the crown.*

[Henry IV Pt. II III I 84]

Nothing left

> *My pride fell with my fortunes*

[As You Like It I ii 124]

Cruel Justice

> *And when he falls,*
> *He falls like Lucifer,*
> *Never to rise again.*

[Henry VIII III ii 450]

So, join the contented majority
Who doth ambition shun,
And loves to lie i'th'sun,
Seeking the food he eats,
And pleas'd with what he gets,
Come hither, come hither, come hither.
Here shall he see
No enemy
But winter and rough weather.

[As You Like It II v 34]

Chapter 38: The After-dinner Speech

The skills that bring about success on the golf course count for little when it comes to the courtesy of acknowledging the fruits of victory. The acceptance speech can be for many a far more daunting task than sinking a vital putt on the last green. This does not apply to the Club Captain of course. Through practice he has become a dab-hand, and regularly produces a tour-de-force to mark even minor occasions in the club diary. Come the club dinner in celebration of his year in office he has therefore mastered the skills of oratory to perfection.- Or has he? W.S. has a few tips.

Cut it!

> *Since brevity is the soul of wit,*
> *And tediousness the limbs and outward flourishes,*
> *Be brief.*

[Hamlet II ii 90]

Know your listeners

> *A jest's prosperity lies in the ear*
> *Of him that hears it, never in the tongue*
> *Of him that makes it.*

[Love's Labour's Lost V ii 869]

Speak with authority

> *When he speaks the air, a chartered libertine, is still.*

[Henry V I i 47]

Avoid pomposity

> *Give me leave to speak my mind*
> *And I will cleanse the foul body of the infected world*
> *If they will patiently receive my medicine*

[As You Like It II vii 57]

Be one of us

> *You speak o'th'people as if you were a god, to punish*
> *Not a man of their of their infirmity.*

[Coriolanus III 1 80]

Not repetitious

> *As tedious as a twice told tale*
> *Vexing the dull ear*
> *Of a drowsy man.*

[King John III iv 108]

Be yourself

> *O'erstep not the modesty of nature; for anything*
> *So overdone is from the purpose.*

> [Hamlet III ii 19]

So don't try this on

> *I come not friends to steal away your hearts.*
> *I am no orator.*

> [Julius Caesar III ii 216]

Or over the top with this

> *I have neither wit, nor words nor worth,*
> *Action nor utterance, nor the power of speech*
> *To stir men's blood. I only speak right on.*

> [Julius Caesar III ii 221]

Not roguish

> *A knavish speech sleeps in a foolish ear.*

> [Hamlet IV ii 22]

Or clever

> *Full of wise saws and modern instances.*

> [As You Like It II vii 156]

Avoid hackneyed French or Latin idioms

> *They have been at a great feast of languages*
> *And stolen the scraps.*

> [Love's Labour's Lost V i 33]

Substance not style

> *I do not much dislike the matter but*
> *The manner of his speech.*

> [Antony and Cleopatra II ii 11]

You're learning

> *What, so brief? 'Tis better than to be tedious.*

> [Richard III I ii 88]

Chapter 39: Hospitality

Measured on the scale of intense rivalry the inter-club golf match is about as inconsequential as beating your eight year old son at dominoes. Not so the subsequent entertainment of your visitors however. It follows a familiar pattern of good food and good wine, consumed in convivial company.

On occasions basic hospitality of this gravy takes off in an impromptu way, gathers momentum, time flies, and before you know it you're having to bring it all to a close - unless of course matters have got a wee bit out of hand.

W.S. knew how to bring order to all such occasions.

Welcome

> *Will you see the players well- bestowed?*
> *Let them be well used; for they are the abstract*
> *And brief Chronicles of the time.*

[Hamlet II ii 516]

Bon appetit!

> *Give them great meals of beef and iron and steel;*
> *They will eat like wolves, and fight like devils.*

[Henry V III vii 516]

Cheers!

> *We'll teach you to drink deep ere you depart.*

[Hamlet I ii 175]

He's over indulged——with the best!

> *A man of unbounded stomach*
> *Ever ranking himself with princes.*

[Henry VIII IV ii 38]

A timely toast

> *Now good digestion wait on appetite*
> *And health on both.*

[Macbeth III iv 38]

Same again!

> *Let's have one other gaudy night;*
> *Call to me all my sad captains;*
> *Fill our bowls once more;*
> *Let's mock the midnight bell.*

[Antony and Cleopatra III xiii 182]

Doubles all round

> *To't luxury, pell mell.*

[King Lear IV vi 116]

We've hardly started

> *Gentlemen, prepare not to be gone*
> *We have a trifling , foolish banquet towards.*

[Romeo and Juliet I ii 125]

Try the club's special brew before you go.

> *Drink it off; and if you had the strength of twenty men,*
> *It would dispatch you straight.*

[Romeo And Juliet V i 79]

A sobering thought.

> *Some consequence now hanging in the stars,*
> *Shall bitterly begin his fearful date*
> *With this night's revels.*

[Romeo and Juliet I iv 107]

Chapter 40: Golf boasts

The inflated ego and retribution are closely linked in all walks of life- On and around the golf course they are in cahoots in a big way- There should be notices posted with health warnings against such overweening indulgence. Nemesis surely lurks in a vast array of hazards, strategically located to trap such vanities. In truth golf braggarts are not all that numerous and few would rate their chances of success higher than to risk in excess of a 20/30/40. pence wager on any Sunday morning friendly. In the playing days of W.S. such lily-livered modesty would have been looked on as a Star Chamber matter.

Open' defiance

> *Come the three corners of the world in arms*
> *And we shall shock them.*

[King John V vii 112]

He's tamed them all?

> *And all the courses of my life do show*
> *I am not in the role of common men.*

[Henry IV Pt.I III i 42]

A challenge from one who's suffered

> *Woot weep, woot fight, woot fast, woot tear thyself?*
> *Woot drink up eisl, eat crocodile? I'll do't.*

[Hamlet V i 268]

Devalued success

> *Whatever praises itself but in the deed*
> *Devours the deed in the praise.*

[Troilus and Cressida II iii 152]

Fancied himself a bit

> *Like a strutting player whose conceit*
> *Lies in his hamstring.*

[Troilus and Cressida I iii 153]

Home truths

> *(Some) swear more performance than they are able.*
> *And yet reserve an ability that they never perform.*

[Troilus and Cressida III ii 81]

Match play-The defining moment

> *The hour is come to end the one of us;*
> *And would to God thy name in arms*
> *Were now as great as mine!*

[Henry IV Pt.I V iv 68]

Who's winning so far?

> *I'll make it greater ere I part from thee,*
> *And all the budding honours on thy crest*
> *I'll crop to make a garland for my head.*

[Henry IV Pt I V iv 75]

This must make him favourite

> *At my nativity*
> *The front of heaven was full of fiery shapes,*
> *Of burning cressets; and at my birth*
> *The frame and huge foundation of the earth*
> *Shaked like a coward.*

[Henry IV Pt I III i 13]

But he's not finished yet

> *But I'll endeavour deeds to match those words.*

[Troilus & Cressida IV v 258]

Living in the past

> *His promises were, as he was , mighty;*
> *But his performance, as he is now, nothing.*

[Henry VIII IV ii 42]

Could be embarrassing at St. Andrews

> *Thou art too rude and bold of voice*
> *Parts that become thee happily enough,*
> *And in such eyes as ours appear not faults*
> *But where thou art not known*
> *Why there they show something too liberal.*

[Merchant of Venice II ii 126]

So make us all happy

> *Allay with some cold drops of modesty*
> *Thy skipping spirit.*

[Merchant of Venice II ii 171]

Chapter 41: Hole in One

For the vast majority of golfers the 'Hole in one's the jewel in the crown. Most accolades in golf are denied to all but a gifted few. These are the golfers who are able to string together enough passable shots to win not only a hole or two but the odd championship to boot. The hole in one, on the other hand can be achieved by the most modest of golfers-It's the one shot in a lifetime when all those mysterious components of the golf swing come together by accident, propelling the ball unerringly on line towards the hole, cut, by the grace of god, on that very path which stops it running across the green and into the sand. Other fortuitous factors can combine to cancel out an outrageous tee shot and achieve the same end. Whatever the components, it's a moment to be treasured.
W.S. has witnessed all kinds.

A just reward
> *A hit, a very palpable hit.*

[Hamlet V ii 295]

Wrought by Providence
> *There's a divinity that shapes our ends,*
> *Rough-hew them how we will.*

[Hamlet V ii 10]

Wretched shot, perfect result
> *Such welcome and unwelcome things at once,*
> *'Tis hard to reconcile.*

[Macbeth IV iii 139]

Apologise? Not likely.
> *I cannot wish the fault undone,*
> *The issue of it being so proper.*

[King Lear I i 16]

Folly pays- sometimes.
> *Our indiscretion sometimes serves us well.*

[Hamlet V ii 8]

It really did happen- believe me
> *Season your admiration for a while*
> *With an attent ear, till I may deliver*
> *Upon the witness of these gentlemen,*
> *This marvel to you.*

[Hamlet I ii 193]

Indescribable
> *Give it an understanding but no tongue.*

[Hamlet I ii 209]

You couldn't write the script.
> *If this were played upon a stage now,*
> *I could condemn it as an improbable fiction.*

[Twelfth Night III iv 142]

You should 'ave seen 'em!
> *They threw their caps*
> *As they would hang them on the horns o' th' moon,*
> *Shouting their emulation.*

[Coriolanus I i 210]

Once in a life time
> *Let Hercules himself do what he may*
> *The cat will mew and dog will have his day.*

[Hamlet V i 293]

Stranger things have happened
> *There are more things in heaven and earth,*
> *Than are dreamt of in your philosophy.*

[Hamlet II i 166]

Chapter 42: If It Works, Don't Fix It

Should you be one of those going through life nursing a permanently modest handicap, it is probably because you are guilty of committing the same mistakes, time and time again. A visit to the Pro is mostly the answer, but not always. The resulting change to grip, stance and swing feels so strange that it's not long before you revert to the bad old ways. What is worse it's a bad old way compounded by a botched correction. So, follow the good old maxim, 'if it aint broke don't fix it'

W.S. who once had a golf lesson philosophises in the same vein.

Ambitious? Forget it
> *Striving for better, oft' we mar what's well.*

[King Lear I iv 346]

Settle for being an 'also ran'
> *And makes us rather bear those ills we have,*
> *Than fly to others that we know not of.*

[Hamlet III i 81]

Or worse follows bad
> *Out of the smoke into the smother.*

[As You Like It I ii 266]

You know it makes sense
> *Repent what's past; avoid what is to come;*
> *And do not spread the compost on the weeds,*
> *To make them ranker.*

[Hamlet III iv 149]

Sleep on it!
> *Golden opinions from all sorts of people,*
> *Which would be worn now in their newest gloss,*
> *Not cast aside so soon.*

[Macbeth I vii 33]

Too much reading is bad for you
> *I do see the very book indeed*
> *Where all my sins are writ.*

[Richard II IV i 274]

Tempted by too much technology?
> *Lord we know not what we are,*
> *But know what we may be.*

[Hamlet IV v 4 1]

So you're learning to live with it?

> *I am satisfied and need no more*
> *Than what I know*

[The Winter's Tale II i 189]

Forget it!

> *To mourn a mischief that is past and gone*
> *Is the next way to draw new mischief on.*

[Othello I iii 209]

It'll all come right in the end

> *What is infirm from your sound parts shall fly.*
> *Health shall live free and sickness freely die.*

[All's Well That Ends Well II i 182]

So, it can wait then?

> *Make you amends next but say, sir,*
> *Is it dinnertime?*

[The Comedy of Errors II ii 52]

Look at it this way

> *He is well paid that is well satisfied*

[Merchant Of Venice IV i 410]

Appendix
Shakespeare on Golf

All the world knows that Shakespeare was its one universal genius; but few have as yet realised his extraordinary knowledge of sport, or the extent of his acquaintance with games. From his familiarity with every practical pursuit, he is by some supposed to have been a lawyer , by others a doctor, a sailor, a schoolmaster, a soldier, a printer, an apothecary, a gipsy, a spiritualist. These are, however, but trivial guesses: and it is not only in such secondary matters as History, Science, Philosophy, or Politics that his marvellous knowledge is seen; but also in the far more important sphere of human interest which concerns the sports and relaxations of the race.

 Probably no-one-not Gervinus or Schmidt – not Cowden – Clarke, or the Bishop of St. Andrews- has ever surmised that Shakespeare was a golfer. Proof, however, is abundant that he was not only a distinguished player, acquainted with all the hazards of the game; but that he knew every peculiarity of the St. Andrews links – that he had experience of all the bunkers , that he was familiar with "Walkinshaw" and the "Elysian Fields," that he sometimes drove into the Burn, that he once did the Long Hole in three, and his lowest score was 82.

It is more than probable that when he visited Scotland as a strolling player, and went to Glammis, Dunsinane, and Forres, collecting material for Macbeth, he also spent some time in the ancient Scottish Capital, and solaced himself, after his labours as a playwright and an actor, by an occasional round of the Links.

His familiarity with the old City by the Sea, his allusions to its Castle, with its "coigns of vantage," and its "temple- haunted martlets."

This castle hath a pleasant seat---etc., are well known to every reader of the Plays. References no less apposite to St. Rule, St. Salvator, and St. Leonards, to the Cathedral, the Priory, and the Colleges, are scattered throughout the tragedies and comedies. It will surprise no one to be told that upwards of one hundred allusions to the noble game are to be found in Shakespeare, and that, he prized Golf more than Archery , or Tennis, or Falconry, or Hunting.

 It is unquestionable that the Game of Golf is a mirror of chief incidents and accidents of life; that, from the opening tee- shot to the final putt, it is a picture of human experience: and, while it may be disputed whether to be a good golfer is necessarily to be a good fellow, every golfing community knows that the play reveals the man, in a very remarkable manner. Hence it was inevitable that, as soon as Shakespeare crossed the Border, he should take to the game, and should dearly love it, both for its own sake and for what it reveals of human nature. The quotations, which follow, are a mere selection from our great dramatist's allusions to the Green, with its incidents and adventures.

Key Words

Audit—How my A stands, who knows save heaven	33 Epitaphs
Augmentation–More lines than the new map with the A of the Indies	10 Club Characters
Avoid—Repent what's past, A what is to come	42 If It Works
Axe—Where the offence is, let the great A fall	22 The Caddie
Babbled—B o'green fields	33 Epitaphs
Bagpiper—And laugh like parrots at a B	10 Club Characters
Banish—B plump Jack and B all the world	10 Club Characters
Banished—For what offence have I this fortnight been a B woman?	23 Golf Widow
Banquet—We have a trifling foolish B towards	39 Hospitality
Bargain—In the way of B I'll cavil on the ninth part of a hair	15 Rules Of Golf
Base—Scorning the B degrees by which he did ascend	10 Club Characters
Bastards—Now God stand up for B	29 Winning Is All
Battalions—When sorrows come, they come not single spies but in B	2 Hazards
Battle—When the B's lost and won	7 End Game
Bawcock—Good B bate thy rage	36 Cool Head
Beef—Great meals of B and iron and steel	39 Hospitality
Beggars—When B die there are no comets seen	7 End Game
Bell—Let's mock the midnight B	39 Hospitality
Bellyful—Rumble thy B. Spit, fire! Spout, rain	26 Foul Weather Golf
Bend—That same eye whose B doth awe the world	4 First Tee
Bestial—Lost the immortal part of myself and what remains is B	32 Self Chastisement
Bethumped—Zounds! I was never so B with words	15 Rules of Golf
Bias—B and thwart not answering the aim	9 Putting
Bitter—'Tis B cold and I am sick at heart	26 Foul Weather Golf
Bladder—A plague of sighing and grief! It blows a man up like a B	2 Hazards
Bladders—Like little wanton boys that swim on B	31 Ambition
Blast—When the B of war blows in our ears	18 The Big Match
Blastments—Contagious B are most imminent	5 Strokes
Blaze—His rash fierce B of riot cannot last	6 Shots
Bleeding—O pardon me thou B piece of earth	11 Etiquette
Blench—If he but B I know my course	3 Gamesmanship
Blessed—This B plot, this other Eden,demi-paradise	8 Nineteenth
Blood—Make thick my B; stop up the access and passage to remorse	31 Game Of Love
--O the B more stirs to rouse a lion than to start a hare	20 A Man's Game
Bloodily—How B the sun begins to peer above yon busky hill	30 Early Morning Golf
Bloody—What B man is that?	12 Abuse
--Be B, bold and resolute	6 Shots
--I do begin to have B thoughts	9 Winning Is All
Blow—B winds and crack your cheeks	26 Foul Weather Golf
Body—When that this B did contain a spirit	33 Epitaphs
Bondman—Who is here so base that would be a B?	22 The Caddie
Bonnet—Put your B to its right use. 'Tis for the head	14 Dress
Book—And now I will unclasp a secret B	15 Rules Of Golf
Bosom—Cleanse the stuffed B of that perilous stuff	1 Golf Lesson
Bounty—The less they deserve, the more merit is in thy B	3 Gamesmanship
Bourne—From whose B no traveller returns	17 Come Here Often
Brain—Raze out the written troubles of the B	1 Golf Lesson
Brains—I have very poor and unhappy B for drinking	24 Ancient Royals
Brandished—Disdaining fortune with his B steel	6 Shots
Brave—O B new world that has such creatures in it	10 Club Characters
Breach—Once more unto the B dear friends, once more	18 The Big Match
--More honoured in the B than the observance	11 Etiquette
--His gashed stabs looked like a B in nature	9 Putting
Breath—The windy suspiration of forced B	19 Body Language
--Hold hard the B and bend up every spirit to its full height	4 First Tee

Eager—It is a nipping and an E air	26 Foul Weather Golf
Ear—Give everyman thine E but few thy voice	3 Gamesmanship
--A jest's prosperity lies in the E of the beholder	38 After Dinner Speech
Earth—Two paces of the vilest E is room enough	33 Epitaphs
Eastern—Walks o'er the dew of yon high E hill	30 Early Morning Golf
--Check'ring the E clouds with streaks of light	30 Early Morning Golf
Easy—An E leap to pluck bright honour from the pale faced moon	34 Honour
--If to do were as E as to know what were good to do	1 Golf Lesson
Ecstasy—Where violent sorrow seems a modern E	2 Hazards
---Blown youth blasted with E	24 Ancient Royals
Eden—This other E, demi paradise	8 Nineteenth
Elements—I tax you not you E, you owe me no subscription	25 Foul Weather Golf
Emulation—On the horns o' the moon, shouting their E	41 Hole In One
Endeavour—Why should our E be so loved	24 Ancient Royals
--I'll E deeds to match those words	40 Golf Boasts
Ended—When remedies are past, the griefs are E	2 Hazards
Endure—Great men great losses should E	16 Philosophisers
Enemies—To know our E' minds we'd rip their hearts	31 Game Of Love
Enforce—So to E or qualify the laws as to your own self seems good	15 Rules Of Golf
Engineer—To have the E hoist with his own petard	3 Gamesmanship
England—All the youth of E are on fire	18 Big Match
--Heaven take my soul and E keep my bones	33 Epitaphs
Enurned—The sepulchre wherein we saw thee quietly E	9 Putting
Epileptic—A plague upon your E visage	12 Abuse Everywhere
--Search E in the high grown field and bring him	17 Come Here Often
Epilogue—A good play needs no E	33 Epitaphs
Error—The E of our eye directs our mind	9 Putting
--O hateful E, melancholy's child	4 First Tee
Eruptions—Diseased nature oftentimes breaks forth in strange E	21 Links Courses
Everything—Sans teeth, sans eyes, sans taste, sans E	24 Ancient Royals
Evil—A gracious voice obscures the show of E	3 Gamesmanship
Excellent—O it is E to have a giant's strength	6 Shots
Execution—That comfort comes too late;'tis like a pardon after E	8 Nineteenth
Extremes—'Twixt two E of passion, joy and grief	7 End Game
Eye—Oft the E deceives, the mind being troubled	9 Putting
--Things in motion sooner catch the E than what not stirs	5 Strokes --I
--I have not from your E that gentleness and show of love	31 Game Of Love
--Come stretch thy chest and let thy E spout blood	18 Big Match
Eyed—The grey E morn smiles on the frowning night	30 Early Morning Golf
Face—Was this a F to be opposed against the warring winds	26 Foul Weather Golf
--I do fear thy F is too full of human kindness	31 Game Of Love
Faint—I have a F cold fear thrills through my veins	9 Putting
Fair—So F and foul a day I have not seen	26 Foul Weather Golf
--Disguise F nature with hard favoured rage	18 Big Match
Faith—She swore in F 'twas strange,'twas passing strange	23 Golf Widow
Fall—That strain again, it had a dying F	19 Body Language
False—To show an unfelt sorrow is an office which the F man does	3 Gamesmanship
Familiar—Then shall our names F in his mouth as household words	8 Nineteenth
Famoused—The painful warrior F for fight	27 Final Farewell
Fancy—So full of shapes is F, that it alone is high fantastical	13 Hanging Fire
Fantasy—Is this not something more than F	5 Strokes
Farewell—F, God knows when we shall meet again	4 First Tee
--F, the tranquil mind, F content	35 Dejection
Fashion—Thou art not for the F of these times	24 Ancient Royals
--His brains still beating, puts him thus from F of himself	9 Putting

Fates—Men at some are masters of their F	23 Golf Widow
Fault—If ought of this miscarry by my F let my old life be sacrificed	22 The Caddie
--If sugar and sack be at F God help the wicked	25 Rub Of The Green
--So may he rest; his F lie gently on him	33 Epitaphs
Condemn the F	6 Shots
Fear—Put on fear and cast yourself in wonder	4 First Tee
--To deal plainly I F I am not in my perfect mind	24 Ancient Royals
Fearing—Lose the good we oft might win by F the attempt	13 Hanging Fire
Fears—Bound in by saucy doubts and F	4 First Tee
Feast—Nature's second course, chief nourisher in life's F	8 Nineteenth
February—What's the matter that you have such a February face?	35 Dejection
Feel—Speak what we F not what we ought to say	16 Philosophisers
Feeling—Apprehension of the good gives the greater F to the worse	28 Consolation
Fell—That no compunctious visitings of nature shake my F purpose	31 Game Of Love
Fellow—This F's wise enough to play the fool	10 Club Characters
Fever—After life's fitful F he sleeps well	33 Epitaphs
Fiery—The flash and outbreak of a F mind	5 Strokes
Fight—Woot wee, woot F, woot fast, woot tear thyself?	40 Golf Boasts
Filches—He that F from me my good name	34 Honour
Filthy—A F, worsted –stocking knave	12 Abuse
Find—You shall F no boy's play here I can tell you	20 A Man's Game
Finding—F ourselves too slow we put on a compelled vigour	11 Etiquette
Fine—Why tell me of moderation, the grief is F	6 Shots
Fire—O for a Muse of F that would ascend the brightest heaven	18 Big Match
--Yoked with a lamb that carries anger as the flint bears F	36 Cool Head
--Spit F, spot rain	26 Foul Weather Golf
--And 'gins to pale his ineffectual F	30 Early Morning Golf
Fires—Violent F soon burn out themselves	66 Shots
Fit—A dish F for the gods	1 Golf Lesson
--You must translate, 'tis F we understand them	1 Golf Lesson
Fish—Thou debosh'd F thou!	12 Abuse
Flat—How weary, stale, F, and unprofitable seem to me all the uses	35 Dejection
Flaws—This heart shall break into a thousand F or ere I'll weep	2 Hazards
Flesh—Buy food and get thyself in F	22 The Caddie
--O that this too too solid F would melt	35 Dejection
Flexible—Makes F the knees of knotted oaks	26 Foul Weather Golf
Flight—Where the F so runs against all reason	5 Strokes
Fling—F away ambition .By that sin fell the angels	37 Ambition
Flood—Which taken at the F leads on to fortune	37 Ambition
Flout—F 'em and scout 'em, and F 'em and scout 'em	15 Rules Of Golf
Flower—Look like the innocent F but be the serpent under't	3 Gamesmanship
Flushing—Had left the F of her galled eyes	23 Golf Widow
Fly—My words F up, my thoughts remain below	9 Putting
Foe—Heat not a furnace for your F so hot that it do singe	31 A game Of Love
Fog—Hover through the F and filthy air	26 Foul Weather Golf
Folly—What F I commit I dedicate to you	25 Rub Of The Green
--Beat at this gate that let thy F in and thy dear judgement out	32 Self Chastisement
Fond—I am a very foolish, F old man	24 Ancient Royals
Fool—Better a witty F than a foolish wit	10 Club Characters
--Thou knotty-pated F	12 Abuse
Foolish—A knavish speech sleeps in a F ear	38 After Dinner Speech
Fore bear—Meantime F, and let mischance be slave to patience	36 Cool Head
Forbid—And therefore I F my tears	2 Hazards
Force—Good reasons must of F give way to better	25 Rub Of The Green
Forced—Like the F gait of a shuffling nag	19 Body Language
Forget—Old men F and all shall be forgot but he'll remember	8 Nineteenth

134

Forgive—F me, I had it from my father	25 Rub Of The Green
Forgot—And all the rest F for which he toiled	27 Final Farewell
Fortnight—For what offence have I this F been a banished woman?	23 Golf Widow
Fortune—And thus my F runs against the bias	25 Rub Of The Green
--The slings and arrows of outrageous F	36 Cool Head
Foul—For nothing can seem F to those that win	29 Winning Is All
Fountain—My mind is troubled like a F stirred	35 Dejection
Frailty—F, thy name is woman	23 Golf Widow
Frame—This goodly F, the earth, seems to me a sterile promontory	35 Dejection
Free—Let your indulgence set me F	27 Final Farewell
Fretful—Like quills upon the F porpentine	7 End Game
Frets—A poor player that struts and F his hour upon the stage	27 Final farewell
Friend—A F should bear his F's infirmities	28 Consolation
Frighted—Shall I be F when a madman stares	36 Cool Head
Frost—A killing F nips his root and then he falls	37 Ambition
--So full of F and storm and cloudiness	35 Dejection
Frowning—The grey-eyed morn smiles on the F night	30 Early Morning Golf
Fulfil—Your purpled hands to reek and smoke F your pleasure	8 Nineteenth
Furious—No more the heat of the sun, nor the F winter's rages	27 Final Farewell
Furlongs—A thousand F of sea	21 Links Courses
Gadding—How now my headstrong, where have you been G	17 Come Here Often?
Gall—I am pigeon-livered and lack G	29 Winning Is All
Galled—Ere yet the flushing in her G eyes	23 Golf Widow
Garland—I'll crop to make a G for my head	40 Golf Boasts
Garlic—I'd rather live with cheese and G	10 Club Characters
Garters—Hang thyself in thine own heir-apparent G	12 Abuse
Gaudy—Rich but not G	14 Dress
--Let's have one other G night	39 Hospitality
Gentle—His life was G and the elements so mixed in him	33 Epitaphs
--There's many a G person made a Jack	10 Club Characters
Gentleness—I have not from your eyes that G and show of love	31 Game Of Love
Giant—Excellent to have G's strength	6 Shots
Gifts—Rich G wax poor when givers prove unkind	22 Caddie
Glove—Why wearest thou that G upon thy cap?	14 Dress
Glow-worm—The G shows the matin to be near	30 Early Morning Golf
Gnaw—Why G you so your nether lip?	19 Body Language
Golden—G girls and lads all must	27 Final Farewell
Golgotha—Bathe in reeking wounds or memorise another G	29 Winning Is All
Goodly—O what a G outside falsehood hath	3 Gamesman ship
Goose—Where got'st thou that G look?	12 Abuse
Grace—He does it with more G	22 The Caddy
Gracious—Seasoned with a G voice	3 Gamesmanship
Grain—May his pernicious soul rot half a G a day	31 Game Of Love
--Which G will grow and which will not	37 Ambition
Grass—Plucking the G to see where sits the wind	4 First Tee
Grating—G so harshly all his days of quiet	24 Ancient Royals
Grave—Ignominy sleep with thee in the G	33 Epitaphs
Greasy—Sweep on you fat and G citizens	11 Etiquette
--Thou whoreson, obscene, G tallow-catch	12 Abuse
Green—Sing all a G willow	23 Golf Widow
--With a G and yellow melancholy	23 Golf Widow
Green-eyed—Beware the G	31 Game of Love4
Greyhounds—I see you stand like G in the slips	4 First Tee
Grief—A plague of sighings and G, it blows a man up	2 Hazards
--What's past help should be past G	7 End Game

Hugger-Mugger—We have done but greenly in H to inter him	2 Hazards
Humanity—They imitated H so abominably	11 Etiquette
Hurl—This look of thine will H my soul from heaven	23 Golf Widow
Hurly-burly—When the H,s done	7 End Game
Hurt—Thou hast not half the power to do me harm as I have to H	31 Game Of Love
Husbands—Let H know their wives have sense like them	23 Golf Widow
Image—How can man then, the I of his maker hope to win by it?	37 Ambition
Imitate—Then I the action of the tiger	18 Big Match
Immortal—I have lost the I part of myself	32 Self chastisement
Inauspicious—Shake the yoke of I stars from this world wearied flesh	2 Hazards
Incorporate—The great vow that did I and make us one	22 Golf Widow
Indiscretion—Our I sometimes serves us well	25 Rub Of The Green
Infects—The nature of bad news I the teller	8 Nineteenth
Infirmity—I of his age, yet he has ever but slenderly known himself	24 Ancient Royals
Injuries—The I that wilful men procure must be their schoolmasters	25 Rub Of The Green
Instances—Full of wise saws and modern I	38 After Dinner Speech
Instruct—The Ills we do their Ills I us so	23 Golf Widow
Instruction—But I will better the I	31 Game Of Love
Intelligence—Say from whence you owe this strange I	1 Golf Lesson
Intent—I have no spur to prick the sides of my I	18 Big Match
Interpretation—I will misquote our looks	3 Gamesmanship
Invent –I some other custom of entertainment	24 Ancient Royals
Invention—Filling their hearers with strange I	8 Nineteenth
--Ascend the brightest heaven of I	18 Big Match
Iron—Give me that mattock and the wrenching I	22 Caddie
Issue—I cannot wish the fault undone, the I of it being so proper	41 Hole In One
Jest—A , of fellow of infinite J, of most excellent fancy	10 Club Characters
Jibes—Where are your J now?	33 Epitaphs
Jocund—And J day stands tiptoe on the misty mountain tops	30 Early Morning Golf
Journeymen—I have thought that nature's J had made men	11 Etiquette
Joy—How much better it is to weep at J than to J at weeping	29 Winning Is All
Joint—The time is out of J, O cursed spite that ever I was born	1 Golf Lesson
Jangled—Like sweet bells J, out of time and harsh	1 Golf Lesson
Jaws—Hath ope'd his ponderous J to cast thee up again	9 Putting
Jealousy—Beware J	31 Game of Love
Judgement—Blest are those whose blood and J are well commingled	9 Putting
--Let me have J	15 Rules Of Golf
Justice—Thou hast within thee undivulged crimes unwhipped of J	9 Putting
--Be assured thou shalt have J	15 Rules Of Golf
Kate—Swear me K like a lady as thou art a good mouth filling oath	23 Golf Widow
Kendal—Three misbegotten knaves in K green came at my back	14 Dress
Kill—Let's K all the lawyers	15 Rules Of Golf
Killing—A K frost nips his root, and then he falls	37 Ambition
Kingdom—When this body did contain a spirit a K for it was too small	33 Epitaphs
Kites—Fatted all the region K with this slave's offal	29 Winning Is All
Knave—A duteous, knee-crooking K	22 Caddie
Knavish—A K speech sleeps in a foolish ear	38 After Dinner Speech
Knocking—Whence is that K? How is't when every noise appals me	13 Hanging Fire
Know—We K what we are, but K not what we may be	37 Ambition
--Than fly to others which we K not of	42 If It Works
--I have much ado to K myself	32 Self Chastisement
Knowest—Speak less than thou K	3 Gamesmanship
Known—He hath ever but slenderly K himself	24 Ancient Royals

Law—In L what plea so tainted and corrupt	3 Gamesmanship
--Let my old life be sacrificed to the full rigour of the severest L	22 Caddie
--You keep on the windy side of the L	15 Rules Of Golf
Leap—More worthy to L in ourselves than to tarry	2 Hazards
Leaving—Nothing in his life became him like the L of it	33 Epitaphs
Left—And there I L him, tranc'd	17 Come Here Often?
Lend—L me ten thousand eyes and I will fill them with prophetic tears	2 Hazards
Lenity—Use L sweet chuck	36 Cool Head
Let—Now L it work, mischief thou art afoot	3 Gamesmanship
--L the doors be shut upon him that he may play the fool	10 Club Characters
Libertine—Like a puff'd and reckless L, himself the primrose path	1 Golf Lesson
Library—Take comfort of all my L	28 Consolation
Life—Fie upon this quiet L, I want work	23 Golf Widow
--So long lives this and this gives L to thee	27 Final Farewell
Light—Check' ring' the eastern clouds with streaks of L	30 Early Morning Golf
Lightest—Whose L word would harrow up my soul	7 End Game
Lightening—Too like the L that hath ceased to be ere one can say	6 Shots
Like—Take him for all in all we shall not see his L again	10 Club Characters
Lines—He doth smile his face into more L than are in the new map	10 Club Characters
Lips—His coward L did from their colour fly	4 First Tee
--This is no world to tilt with mammets and to play with L	20 A Man's Game
Little—Though she is but L she is fierce	23 Golf Widow
Little—Better for being a L bad	28 Consolation
Liver—If he were opened and you find so much blood in his L	12 Abuse
Loathed—Our performance so L	24 Ancient Royals
Locks—Pluck up drowned honour by the L	34 Honour
Lodge—The thorns that in her bosom L to prick and sting her	23 Golf Widow
Longings—I have immortal L in me	37 Ambition
Look—L on't again, I dare not	9 Putting
Looks—Let not our L put on our purpose	3 Gamesmanship
--L quite through the deeds of men	10 Club Characters
Loon—Thou cream-faced L	12 Abuse
Loosed—As if he had been L out of Hell	4 First Tee
Losers—Then with the L let it sympathise	29 Winning Is All
Loses—Who L, who wins, who's in, who's out	8 Nineteenth
Loss—Wise men ne'er sit and wail their L	16 Philosophisers
Losses—Great men, great L should endure	16 Philosophisers
--Glancing an eye of pity on his L	28 Consolation
Lost—I have L my reputation	32 Self Chastisement
Love—The rites for which I L him are bereft me	23 Golf Widow
--Do not presume too much upon my L	23 Golf Widow
Loves—A gentleman that L to hear himself talk	10 Club Characters
Lunacy—Days of quiet with turbulent and dangerous L	14 Ancient Royals
Lustre—That eye, whose bend doth awe the world did lose its L	19 Body Language
Luxury—To't L pell-mell	39 Hospitality
Mad—Go to, I'll no more on't, it hath made me M	12 Abuse
Made—Where shrieks that rend the air are M	Hazards
--What stuff 'tis M of I know not	35 Dejection
Madness—With a crafty M keeps aloof, when we would bring him on	13 Hanging Fire
--This is very Midsummer M	6 Shots
Majestical—We do it wrong, being M, to offer it the show of violence	5 Strokes
Malice—Nothing extenuate, nor set down aught in M	33 Epitaphs
Mankind—A tenth of M would hang themselves	23 Golf Widow
Manner—I do not like so much the matter but the M of his speech	38 After Dinner Speech
Mantle—The morn in russet M clad	30 Early Morning Golf

139

Nature—So far hath discretion fought with N	6 Shots
--N In you stands on the very verge of her confine	24 Ancient Royals
--That N might stand up and say to all the world	33 Epitaphs
--Losses that Ns fragile vessel doth sustain	24 Ancient Royals
--N hath framed strange fellows in her time	10 Club Characters
Necessity—As if we were villains of N	25 Rub Of The Green
Need—O reason not the N	6 Shots
Needed—What N then that terrible dispatch	5 Strokes
Needful—Leaves unquestioned matters of N value	11 Etiquette
Nettle—Out of this N danger we pluck this flower	6 Shots
Nimbly—The air N recommends itself to our gentle senses	30 Early Morning Golf
Nipping—It is a N and an eager air	30 Early Morning Golf
Nobler—Whether 'tis N in the mind to suffer	36 Cool Head
North—Thou art now sailed into the N of my lady's opinion	23 Golf Widow
Nose—His N was as sharp as a pen	33 Epitaphs
Nothing—N is either good or bad but thinking makes it so	4 First Tee
--He speaks an infinite deal of N	10 Club Characters
Nunnery—.Get thee to a N	12 Abuse
Oaks—Make flexible the knees of knotted O to part	26 Foul Weather Golf
Oath—A good mouth filling O	23 Golf Widow
Obey—The weight of this sad time we must O	16 Philosophisers
Oblivion—Strewed with husks and formless ruin of O	16 Philosophisers
--Second childishness and mere O	24 Ancient Royals
Obscene—O and greasy tallow-catch	12 Abuse
Observance—More honoured in the breach than the O	11 Etiquette
Observed—The O of all observers, quite, quite down	1 Golf Lesson
Observer—He is a great O and looks quite through the deeds of men	1 Club Characters
O'er—A south-west blow on ye and blister ye all O	12 Abuse
O'erleaps—Vaulting ambition O itself	37 Ambition
Offence—O my O is rank	32 Self Chastisement
--It is not meet that every nice O should bear this C	12 Abuse
Offences—More O at my back than I have thoughts to put them in	32 Self Chastisement
Offices—Thou better knowest the O of nature	23 Golf Widow
Old—Poor O man, as full of grief as age	24 Ancient Royals
--Thou should'st not have been O till thou had'st been wise	24 Ancient Royals
Once—Stand not upon the order of your going, but go at O	11 Etiquette
One –Scraped O out of the table	15 Rules Of Golf
Opinion—The gross and scope of my O	21 Links Courses
Oppose—To O the bolt against my coming in	23 Golf Widow
Opposing—And by O, end them	36 Cool Head
Oppressors—The O wrong, the proud man's contumely	22 Caddie
Orator—I am no O	38 After Dinner Speech
Ornament—That which thou esteem'st the O of life	6 Shots
Other—Either say thou'lt do it, or thrive by O means	20 A Man's Game
Others—Than fly to O that we know not of	42 If It Works
Ourselves—To find O dishonourable graves	10 Club Characters
Overdone—Anything so O is from the purpose	11 Etiquette
Paces—Two P of the vilest earth is room enough	33 Epitaphs
Pains—She gave me for my P a world of sighs	23 Golf Widow
Palaces—Poor men's cottages, Princes P	1 Golf Lesson
Palates—P both for sweet and sour	23 Golf Widow
Pale—Look P and gaze and put on fear	4 First Tee
Palpable—A hit, a very P hit	41 Hole In One
Paper—The unpleasantest words that ever blotted P	15 Rules Of Golf

Part—I'll cavil on the ninth P of a hair	15 Rules Of Golf
--I hold it meet that we shake hands and P	7 End me
--Thy knotted locks to	7 End Game
--For mine own P, it was Greek to me	15 Rules Of Golf
Parts—Affliction is enamoured of thy P	2 Hazards
Particular—And each P hair to stand on end	7 End Game
Parting—Why then this P was well made	4 First Tee
Passeth—I have that which P show	14 Dress
Passion—Twixt two extremes of P, joy and grief	7 End Game
--Give that man that is not Ps slave and I will wear him	36 Cool Head
--Tear a P to tatters	38 After Dinner Speech
Pastors—Do not as some ungracious P do	1 Golf Lesson
Pat—Now might I do it P	3 Gamesmanship
Pated—A rumbustious, Periwig-P fool	38 After Dinner Speech
Patience—Like P on a monument smiling at grief	23 Golf Widow
Perform—What needful else we will P in measure time and place	3 Gamesmanship
Performance—Swear more P than they are able	40 Golf Boasts
Pernicious—May his P soul rot	31 A Game Of Love
Perturbed—Rest, rest P spirit	9 Putting
Perusal—He fell to such P of my face	1 Golf Lesson
Petard—To have the engineer hoist with his own P	3 Gamesmanship
Petty—We P men walk under his huge legs and peep about	10 Club Characters
Phantasma—like a P or a hideous dream	13 Hanging Fire
Philosophy—Than are dreamt of in your P	41 Hole In One
Pierce—Shall P thy slimy jaws	5 Strokes
Pinched—With a kind of colic P and vexed	21 Links Courses
Pinching—How in this our P cave shall we discourse	26 Foul Weather Golf
Pined—She P in thought	23 Golf Widow
Pious—With devotion's visage and P action	3 Gamesmanship
Pirate—Like the sanctimonious P who went to sea	15 Rules Of Golf
Piteous—He raised a sigh so P and profound	2 Hazards
Pith—Enterprises of great P and moment with this regard	12 Hanging Fire
Pity—Is there no P sitting in the clouds that sees into the bottom	2 Hazards
Pitiful—'Twas P, 'twas wondrous P	23 Golf Widow
Place—Screw your courage to the sticking P and we'll not fail	4 First Tee
Plain—I will a P, unvarnished tale deliver	8 Nineteenth
Plague—The red P rid you for learning me your language	27 Final Farewell
Play—That's all one, our P is done	7 End Game
Played—If this were P upon a stage now I could condemn it	41 Hole In One
Players—Will you see the P well bestowed	39 Hospitality
Pleasance—Youth is full of P, age is full of care	24 Ancient Royals
Pleasure—While your purple hands do reek and smoke, fulfil your P	8 Nineteenth
--Dwell I within the suburbs of your P?	23 Golf Widow
Pleasures—'Tis not in thee to grudge my P	23 Golf Widow
Plummet—Deeper than did ever P sound, I'll drown my book	7 End Game
Ponderous—Hath op'd his P jaws to cast thee up again	9 Putting
Pontic—Like to the P sea, whose icy current and compulsive course	31 Game Of Love
Potatoes—Let the sky rain P	26 Foul Weather Golf
Poverty—My P, but not my will consents	22 Caddie
Power—Thou hast not half the P to do me harm as I have to hurt	31 Game Of Love-
--The P of speech to stir men's blood	38 After Dinner Speech
Praising—P what is lost makes the remembrance dear	3 Gamesmanship
Pray—I P you, being weak , seem so	6 Shots
--For mine own part look you, I'll go P	7 End Game
Prepare—If you have tears P to shed them now	4 First Tee
Presume—Do not P too much upon my love	23 Golf Widow

Sciatica—Which of your hips has the most profound S?	11 Etiquette
Scorning—S the base degrees by which he did ascend	37 Ambition
Scorns—Who would bear the whips and S of time	22 Caddie
Search—S everywhere in the high grown field and bring him	17 Come Here Often?
Service—I have done the state some S , and they know it	33 Epitaphs
Shank—A world too wide for his shrunk S	14 Dress
Shun—That way madness lies, let me S that	6 Shots
Sickness— 'Tis very like he has the falling S	19 Body Language
Sights—There's two or three of us have seen strange S	14 Dress
Sinews—And you my S grow not instant old	9 Putting
--Stiffen the S, summon up the blood	18 The Big Match
Singe—Heat not a furnace for yourself so hot that it do S yourself	31 Game Of Love
Sinning—I am a man more sinned against than S	25 Rub Of The Green
Slip—Let S the dogs of war	18 Big Match
Smile—If we do meet again why we shall S	4 First Tee
Smoke—Out of the S into the smother	2 Hazards
Southerly—When the wind is S I know a hawk from a handsaw	26 Foul Weather Golf
Spared—I could have better S a better man	33 Epitaphs
Spat—You S upon me Wednesday last	31 Game Of Love
Speak—S the speech I pray you, trippingly	38 After Dinner Speech
Spite--O cursed S that ever I was born to set it right	1 Golf Lesson
--Luck in very S of cunning bade him win all	29 Winning Is All
Sport—Hours be short, till fields and blows and groans applaud our S	18 Big Match
Sports—He is given to S, wildness and much company	10 Club Characters
Spot—Look, with a S I damn him	29 Winning Is All
Springes—S to catch woodcocks	3 Gamesmanship
Sprites—Rise up and walk like S to countenance this horror	5 Strokes
Spurned—You S me such a day, another time you called mw dog	31 A game Of Love
Stage—A S where every man must play a part and mine a sad one	35 Dejection
Star Chamber—Ill make a S C matter of it	15 Rules Of Golf
Steep—Show me the S and thorny way to Heaven	1 Golf Lesson
Stomach—He which hath no S to this fight, let him depart	18 Big Match
Storms—Small showers last long, but sudden S are short	6 Shots
Strange—She swore in faith 'twas S, 'twas passing S	23 Golf Widow
--Misery acquaints a man with S bedfellows	8 Nineteenth
Strangers—I do desire we may be better S	29 Winning Is All
Straw—What art thou that dost grumble there i'the S?	17 Come Here Often
Strewed—What's past and what's to come is S with husks	16 Philosophisers
Strife—Pursue me lasting S	23 Golf Widow
Strings—The S of life began to crack, and there I left him	17 Come Here Often?
Striving—S for better, oft we mar what's well	42 If It Works
Strokes—Good words are better than bad S	12 Abuse
Strutting—Like a S player whose conceit lies in his hamstring	40 Golf Boasts
Sulphur—Roast me in S,	32 Self Chastisement
Summon—S up the blood	18 Big Match
--S up remembrance of things past	27 Final Farewell
Sun—Fear no more the heat of the S	27 Final Farewell
Suspiration—The windy S of forced breath	19 Body Language
Swallows--It engluts and S other sorrows	2 Hazards
Sway—When all the S of earth shakes like a thing unfirm	26 Foul Weather Golf
Sweet—Shall serve for S discourses in our times to come	2 Hazards
--Sweets to the S, farewell	2 Hazards
Swift—Too S arrives as tardy as too slow	11 Etiquette
Tainted—In law, what plea so T and corrupt	3 Gamesmanship
Tale—I will a plain, unvarnished T deliver	8 Nineteenth

145

Violent—V fires soon burn out themselves ... 6 Shots
　　　　—V delights have V ends ... 33 Epitaphs for Golfers
Virtue—Assume a V if you have it not ... 3 Gamesmanship
Visitation—This V is but to Whet thy almost blunted purpose ... 1 Golf Lesson
Voice—Her V was ever soft, gentle and low, an excellent thing ... 23 Golf Widow
Voyage—In life's uncertain V I will some kindness do them ... 24 Ancient Royals
　　　　—All the V of their life is bound in shallows and in miseries ... 37 Ambition

Wages—Home art gone and ta'en thy W ... 33 Epitaphs
Wasted—I W time, and doth time waste me ... 33 Epitaphs
Wages—Home art gone and ta'en thy W ... 33 Epitaphs
Wasted—I W time, and doth time waste me ... 33 Epitaphs
Watch—He's winding up the W of his wit, by and by, it will strike ... 10 Club Characters
Weak—I pray you, being W, seem so ... 6 Shots
Weary—So W with disasters that I would set my life on any chance ... 2 Hazards
Weaved—Ill-W ambition, how much art thou shrunk ... 7 End Game
Wednesday—You spat upon me W last ... 31 Game Of Love
Weep—Woot W, woot fight, woot fast? ... 40 Golf Boasts
Welcome—Such W and unwelcome things at once ... 41 Hole In One
Whirligig—The W of time brings in his revenges ... 29 Winning Is All
Whirling—These are wild and W words ... 12 Abuse
Whistle—W her off and let her down the wind ... 4 First Tee
Wither—Age cannot W her ... 23 Golf Widow
Widow—If once a W ever I be a wife ... 23 Golf Widow
Willow—Sing all a green W ... 23 Golf Widow
Wind—Sits the W in that quarter? ... 22 Caddie
Winds–Blow W and crack your cheeks ... 26 Foul Weather Golf
　　　　—Was this a face to be opposed against the warring W? ... 26 Foul Weather Golf
Winter—Here shall you see no enemy, but W and rough weather ... 26 Foul Weather Golf
Wise—This fellow's W enough to play the fool ... 10 Club Characters
Wit—Better a witty fool than a foolish W ... 10 Club Characters
Wits—It strains me past the compass of my W ... 6 Shots
Wives—Should all despair that have revolted W ... 23 Golf Widow
Words—W without thoughts never to heaven go ... 9 Putting
Work—Now let it W, mischief thou art afoot ... 3 Gamesmanship
World—The W is full of rubs, my fortune runs against the bias ... 25 Rub Of The Green
　　　　—Stale, flat and unprofitable seem to me all the uses of this W ... 35 Dejection
Worse—And W I may be yet ere one can say this is the worst ... 7 End Game
Wretched—Full of grief as age, W in both ... 24 Ancient Royals
Wrong—If you W us shall we not revenge? ... 31 Game Of Love

Yarn—A mingled Y, good and ill together ... 8 Nineteenth
Yellow—My way of life is fall'n into the sear and Y leaf ... 24 Ancient Royals
　　　　—Who commended thy Y stockings? ... 14 Dress
Yoked—Y with a lamb that carries anger as the flint bears fire ... 36 Cool Head
Youth—That unmatched figure of blown Y ... 24 Ancient Royals

147

ISBN 1-41205476-1